To my family of German descent

Photograph of immigrants
Peter Johann Happel & Katharina Elisabeth Werning

GENEALOGICAL GUIDE
TO TRACING ANCESTORS
IN GERMANY

Margaret Krug Palen

HERITAGE BOOKS
2007

HERITAGE BOOKS

AN IMPRINT OF HERITAGE BOOKS, INC.

Books, CDs, and more—Worldwide

For our listing of thousands of titles see our website
at
www.HeritageBooks.com

Published 2007 by
HERITAGE BOOKS, INC.
Publishing Division
65 East Main Street
Westminster, Maryland 21157-5026

Other books by the author:
Genealogical Research Guide to Germany
German Settlers of Iowa: Their Descendants, and European Ancestors
German Settlers of Iowa: Their Descendants, and European Ancestors, Revised Edition

International Standard Book Number: 978-0-7884-0280-7

Contents

Illustrations

Acknowledgements

Permission to reproduce German Costume Plates A through H granted by Rheingauer Verlagsgesellschaft, Eltville am Rhein, Germany.

Löhlbach Forester Hermann Simon and his wife, Edda, photographed parish registers and assisted in research.

A special thanks to Jetta Ollek for contributing German family record illustrations.

Introduction

Why should you trace your ancestral past and hunt for your roots in Germany? A name traced through centuries is worth more than life's riches according to the Bible, Proverbs 22:1. A name of ancient inheritance is a treasure to be valued. Man has an innate desire to find out where he came from. Perhaps this is why a growing number of people are digging into their Germanic pasts to find ancestors. In Germany the past is honored and preserved and there is often much for the genealogy researcher to discover.

Many genealogy searchers today are about 55 years of age, though more and more younger and professional people are getting involved in tracking ancestors. They are learning what their ancestors did, how they earned a living, how they dressed, what food they ate, and what was happening in history at the time of emigration from Germany. They even find clues to why ancestors left their homeland. Time and patience are required to discover all that, but the reward of understanding family life is worth the effort to connect the present with the past.

German people are the largest ethnic group in the United States of America. About 55 million Americans of German descent reside in the fifty states. This volume contains a description of the land of Germany and its history with important dates that may have a bearing on family history. Searching genealogy backward through the centuries makes it increasingly important for the researcher to have a working knowledge of German history.

I began my journey into my ancestral past at a young age without realizing it at the time. Grandfather's first language was German and he rarely spoke English, his second language. I listened with great interest whenever Grandpa spoke in English and remembered what he said. My generation is the first of our large extended German family to have English as the first language, and every effort was made to make sure we did not learn German. The only time Grandpa spoke in English was when he described the family homeland in Germany. I never forgot Grandpa's description of Löhlbach and Altenhaina Kreiss, Frankenburg, Provinz Hessen Nassau, Prussia. Mother recorded what Grandpa said, and her records verified my memory many years later.

My first visit to Germany revealed Grandpa Krug's account of our homeland in Germany was historically accurate. He gave an exact description of the village, county, state and history of Germany at the time the Krug family emigrated to America. However, it was impossible to realize those truths until I made the journey in person to our Old Country village.

The beginning of my search to find the native village of my family on a pull-down wall map of Germany in an elementary school classroom was unsuccessful. The village areas of Germany were not shown on the large map. It was forty years later that I acquired a map showing the small villages in the state of Hessen, Germany. My German surname and Grandpa's family stories about moving from the middle of Germany to the middle of America made it possible to locate my family roots in the Old Country.

When there is not an elder member of the family to assist with family history, much patience and determination will be required to cope with the frustration, obstacles and dead ends one meets when tracing ancestors. Perseverance is an absolutely necessary key ingredient in searching German roots.

Your experience of tracing ancestors may be like that of one researcher tracing a German paternal family in New York, who was able to locate their existence in the United States as early as the 1600s. Or, it may be like that of another who delved into the mystery of family roots and landed in eighth-century France with Emperor Charlemagne, one of the great military leaders of the Middle Ages. Another searcher working on family history wound up in Germany in the 1600s; while another researcher was excited just to find an ancestor who rode with Theodore Roosevelt's "Rough Riders."

Yesterday still lives in the rds of the past. Searching one's roots is not cultural ancestor worship. It is ancestor interest involving an understanding of the history of a locality and country. Anyone fortunate to have German ancestors will find German history interesting and will discover it goes way back into antiquity. There is much to comprehend and learn about Germany.

Tracing a family line exposes the fact that problems are as old as history. Centuries ago it was said that European families should have four children, two to perpetuate the race, one to be lost to war, and one to disease. The idea that human beings, unlike other creatures, should expect all of their offspring to survive is relatively new. It developed within this author's lifetime with the discovery of antibiotics and other sophisticated medicines, then grew to include survival of the infirm and the maimed, and all those who in previous generations would have fallen by the wayside.

All genealogists, whether amateur or professional, share the same interest: digging into their personal pasts to find out who their ancestors were, the length of their life span and cause of demise when known. Genealogy is history on a personal basis. Longer life spans and the quest for the best possible quality of life today require medical histories with information that can only be found in the genetic implications of genealogy research. Many genetically carried diseases in families have been identified including glaucoma, diabetes, muscular dystrophy, hemophilia, Parkinson's disease, some forms of anemia, etc. Preventative medical treatment depends upon what the patient knows about generations of family lineage. Medical diagnosis places great value on a family history of illnesses and causes of death found in genealogy records. It is not difficult to trace and gather this information back several generations.

The recent surge in interest in genealogy also has spread throughout Europe. German villagers wonder what happened to the former inhabitants who emigrated in waves to the New World in the eighteenth and nineteenth centuries. Return genealogical visits to ancestral homelands give rise to additional information that villagers seek about family lineage. Grandmother Happel's relatives in Germany, upon learning of their American family's interest in genealogy, searched the history of a 1936 Happel reunion held in Germany to connect family lineage for almost a thousand years.

It's fun to be an amateur genealogist. It's just like being a detective with a mystery to solve. In the process one meets many other people working on the same problems, the same mysteries. Time is an important requirement in genealogy work, especially when searching in Germany. As genealogical findings progress, it is very exciting to discover things about family, ancestors and descendants. Tracing family roots may not lead to famous people or famous events in history, but for the real genealogy buff any find from the past can be exciting. New discoveries are based on known information. Detective work makes the family tree begin to blossom and family history begins to be treasured. The length of time required to make genealogical progress makes any find an even greater treasure. Whatever is found, genealogy work brings unique insights and pleasures.

Family history can even be combined with interior decorating to beautify the home. Portraits of ancestors, china passed down through generations, and maps of family land add sentimental value to a home decorated in the "Americana" style. Even when the background of old pieces is unknown, they can become treasured heirlooms.

Two hundred years of American history make it possible for all domestic genealogy searchers to trace to the pioneer past. It is fascinating to learn stories of pioneer ancestors. Old cemeteries are a real chronicle of the people of an area. The "high and mighty" lie side by side with the meek and lowly. Death makes them equal.

It doesn't take long for a genealogy buff to find many reminders of those who lived in earlier years. Most people are so busy living in the present that they don't take enough time to look back. That's why digging into genealogy becomes so fascinating. Over a period of time genealogy research adds to a sense of wonder making it so indestructible that it lasts throughout a lifetime and becomes an unfailing antidote against preoccupation with things that are artificial. It can even prevent alienation from the sources of a person's strength.

The unification of East Germany and West Germany into one single nation gave rise to rewriting this research guide to update genealogical sources and methods. Unified Germany increases the possibility of tracing German ancestry with a greater degree of accuracy than could be accomplished for many years. It is possible to continue the search to discover ancestry that no doubt is as old as civilization. German searching brings to the researcher the humbling reality of being a mere link in a very long chain of humanity.

Travel in Israel and the holy city of Jerusalem increased my understanding of Jewish records, Holocaust victims, and consanguinity, the marriage of close relatives found commonly among Jews and Germans of past generations. It also increased my understanding of the history of Germany and the values of German people in both Europe and America.

This volume was written to provide a guide for the aspiring German genealogy buff as well as the more experienced researcher interested in tracing ancestors in Germany. Every German family may have different circumstances to research, therefore, a reference is necessary. This edition is designed as a tool to assist librarians in public libraries or genealogical societies in answering requests from patrons inquiring about researching German ancestors. The genealogical suggestions and methods contained herein are an outgrowth of many years of research in Germany. They encourage families of German descent to evaluate their family heritage, and continue genealogical experiences that preserve family history for future generations.

Margaret Krug Palen

Map of Germany

GERMANY

DENMARK

BALTIC SEA

NORTH SEA

Kiel

SCHLESWIG-HOLSTEIN

Rostock

MECKLENBURG

Hamburg

Schwerin

Bremen

LOWER SAXONY

POLAND

Potsdam   BERLIN

NETHERLANDS

Hannover

Magdeburg

BRANDENBURG

Münster

NORTH RHINE-WESTPHALIA

SAXON-ANHALT

Düsseldorf

Kassel

Weimar

Leipzig

Dresden

Cologne

Marburg

Erfurt

SAXONY

BEL.

Koblenz

THURINGIA

HESSE

Frankfurt

LUX.

Wiesbaden

RHINELAND-PALATINATE

Mainz

Würzburg

CZECHOSLOVAKIA

SAAR

Saarbrucken

Nuremberg

Stuttgart

BAVARIA

FRANCE

BADEN-WURTTEMBERG

Munich

AUSTRIA

SWITZERLAND

[1]

About Germany

Germany, a nation of north-central Europe with an area of 137,768 square miles is bounded on the north by the North Sea, Denmark, and the Baltic Sea; on the east by Poland, Czechoslovakia, and Austria; on the south by Austria, Liechtenstein, and Switzerland; and on the west by France, Luxembourg, Belgium, the Netherlands, and the North Sea. The two states into which Germany was divided in 1949, the Federal Republic of Germany (West Germany) and the German Democratic Republic (East Germany), unified on October 3, 1990 into one nation after the Berlin Wall separating East and West came down November 9, 1989.

The three main physical characteristics of Germany are: various spurs of the Alps that project into Bavaria; a region of secondary mountains with central highlands extending northward from the Alps; and, a region of lowlands sloping generally toward the North and Baltic Seas. The principal ports of Germany, Bremen and Hamburg, are located inland, on the estuaries of rivers. The Bavarian Alps create a natural barrier on the south portion of Germany profoundly influencing the political history of the nation. Germany has an extensive network of rivers, most belonging to the basins of the Baltic and North seas, linked by a system of artificial canals. Canals were the main method of transportation in the Middle Ages in Europe. The Moselle, Main, Elbe and Rhine Rivers make up the German national inland-waterway system. The Rhine River, which forms part of the border with France, is navigable from its mouth in the Netherlands to Basel, Switzerland.

The climate of Germany is influenced by moist, warm winds from the Atlantic Ocean. The western part of Germany has fairly mild winters and summers; eastern Germany has climatic conditions typical of the continental interior of Europe where long, cold winters and short, hot summers prevail. Rainfall is quite evenly distributed throughout the country with 30 to 40 inches occurring in the western and southern highlands.

Germany has many natural resources. The forests of Germany are mentioned prominently in the folklore and mythology of the early Germans. The German word *Wald*, meaning forest, appears in the names of many of the dominant features in the highland region of the central and southern parts of the country, and in areas scattered throughout the lowland region. German flora consists of more than two-thousand flowering plants and mosses; wild fauna includes red and roe deer, wild boar, wolf, fox, wildcat, weasel, marten, otter, and badger; migratory birds include finch, stork, bustard and snow goose.

Germany is not a homogeneous nation. Her people are diverse in culture and languages. The German language, belonging to the Teutonic subfamily of Indo-European languages, has two main dialects, High German and Low German. It is a nasal and guttural language, louder and more vigorous than English. Sound shifts occur and the principal accent falls regularly upon the first syllable of a word except in verbal combinations when the root syllable, not the prefix, is stressed. There are three genders, four cases, a strong and weak declension of adjectives, and an inverted word order. The verb is usually found at the end of the sentence. The German language is constantly modernizing in Germany, therefore, it is necessary to recognize archaic German words in genealogy research and discover new words which are combinations of as many as three or more words. The new words may not be listed in a German dictionary, and to determine the meaning it is necessary to research each part of the word.

The prominent religions of Germany are Lutheran, Roman Catholic, Reformed or Evangelical denominations, and Judaism. An influx of immigrants from the Middle East has increased the number of Eastern religions existing in Germany.

Germany's cultural excellence includes music that has a long history, reaching its height during the eighteenth century. Some of her illustrious composers were: Johann Sebastian Bach, George Frederick Handel, Robert Schumann, Johannes Brahms, Felix Mendelssohn, Richard Wagner, and Richard Strauss. Germany has long been a leader in opera, and has many fine opera houses. The Berlin Philharmonic Orchestra, Hamburg State Orchestra, and Munich Philharmonic Orchestra are renowned internationally.

The source of Germany's wealth for many centuries centered around agricultural enterprises. Due to the growing demands of the population and the Industrial Revolution in the late nineteenth century and the first decade of the twentieth century, the national economy changed. It now was fueled by the mining and refining of iron ores acquired from Alsace-Lorraine, coal, hydroelectric power, and potash required for the production of chemicals. In 1871 Germany was the second largest coal producer in Europe and was at the forefront of the electrical industry. Germany surpassed every nation in industrial and commercial development, but territorial and economic losses resulting from World Wars I and II had a significant impact on the economy. Serious food shortages were caused by separation from the grain-producing areas of East Germany during the postwar recovery of a divided Germany. Aid received from the United States through the European Recovery Program successfully rehabilitated and strengthened the economy. By the late 1950's the German standard of living exceeded the pre-World War II level.

The German culture continues to value the past and there are many castles, historic churches, cathedrals, and museums throughout the country. Evidence of German village people of bygone years can still be found in the traditional costumes preserved over generations by families and museums, and worn at present-day festivals. Costume variations existed in each area of Germany and collections include the practical gear for everyday use as well as Sunday or festival styles. An example of what may be seen in Germany today is that of the state of Hessen where the oldest and simplest costume worn by both sexes was a loose-fitting tunic called the "Saxon Smock" (Fig. A, page 6). Note the smock worn in Thuringia in the illustration, page 10. Variations of the smock are still worn today in many cultures of the world.

The Sunday costume for men in Hessen (Fig. B, page 6) in the seventeenth and eighteenth centuries was a long, dark-colored coat which went to the knees, had light blue or white lining, pockets and wide cuffs, and was decorated with rows of yellow metal buttons. Pants of dark cloth were fastened with four metal buttons, and a cloak reached below the knee. Vests were of dark-colored material lined with rows of metal buttons; the shirt collar was turned down over a black silk neckscarf. White or light blue stockings and dark blue wool leggings were worn; black leather shoes with tongues adorned with silver buckles or leather strings covered the feet. For a head covering, men wore broad-brimmed hats of black felt. For work, village men generally dressed in coarse handwoven linen with a lightweight coat called a *kittel* (extending to the knees), and a knitted woolen stocking cap. On working days, young men wore a blue linen overshirt and a small round black felt hat.

Women wore frocks of dark-colored and self-trimmed linen cloth or thick "linsey-woolsey" skirts with pleats that hung to the calf of the leg (Fig. C, page 6). Hessen women wore many petticoats, reportedly as many as fourteen layers! Each layer was worn above the other, causing the top one to look shorter. Many layers prevented the skirt of black wool, moderately pleated, reaching in length to the calf, from falling straight down and also broke falls when folk dancing was fast and sometimes wild (Fig. E, page 8). Colorful embroidered trimmings and silk ribbons adorned young maidens' Sunday clothing, giving an effulgent and fresh look (See illustrations, page 7 and Fig. H, page 9). After marriage, young matrons continued wearing the same colorful costume until the next death in the family;

from then on, the costume was made of more somber colors. The shirt was either blue or black (white for a dance) (Fig. E, page 8), and sleeves reached down to the elbows. It was common for the women working in their homes to wear the shirt with sleeves rolled up to the elbows (Fig. G, page 9).

Hessen women wore a high bodice or camisole of dark-colored wool or velvet, covering the main part of the back and sides of the upper part of the body. It was fastened to the upper part of the under-skirt and closed in front with two rows of buttons or tied by traversing cords over a bib called a "chest cloth". The chest cloth was made of colorful embroidery or damask linen with colored flowers (Fig. C, page 6). The apron was made of dark blue linen, sometimes striped, and sewn with wide plates designed to go around to the back. Close to the seams were sewn two squares of metallic embroidery or colorful tinsel; the embroidery was attached to a piece of layered fabric or cardboard and was only sewn on the apron when there was a festive occasion to attend. The apron of young girls attending a dance was white. Over their shoulders, women wore a black or dark-colored wool challis neck scarf of colorful print flowers or embroidery bordered with a fringe and folded in a triangle pulled to the front and fastened loosely near the waistline (Fig. G and H, page 9).

Hessen village women wore their hair combed severely upward and twisted into a black quilted silk headcover called an *Abendmahlshaube*; a bow with long, broad ribbon streamers was fastened to the back of the headdress (Fig. D, page 6). The wearing of the *Abendmahlshaube* and dark-colored clothing (Fig. D, page 6) to Sunday Communion services represented symbolically the Christian confession of the female population. A high value was placed on the head covering because it identified which class the women belonged to, also made them look prettier and more attractive.

Stockings of both men and women were of white wool. Triangle-pattern designs were often worn (Fig E and F, page 8). Garters were decorated with silk ribbons or red woolen pompoms that hung from the knee and swung with the movement of the legs (Fig. C, page 6). Black leather shoes were decorated with buckles (Fig. E and F, page 8). Note the buckled shoes worn by men of Thuringia, page 10. Young girls wore black leather cut-out shoes designed with black ribbon rosettes (Fig. H, page 9).

For special occasions, weddings, and dances, young men and boys in some German villages wore white pants and blue jackets (Fig. F, page 8). On Sundays and at festivals, young men wore green or red caps made of velvet and gold cord or tassels decorated with animal fur. The white embroidered shirt collar worn over a silk necktie was decorated with gold and silver embroidery (Fig. F, page

8). Over the shirt, a vest with standup collar made of Merino wool was decorated with colorful stitchery, gold and patterned buttons, blue ribbons, and a cord design. Over the vest a second vest was worn which was a little bit longer and of dark blue cloth; the corners, pocket flaps and back were stitched with blue silk in a floral pattern. Each side had a row of patterned metal buttons. This overvest was collarless. A jacket, worn over both vests, (Fig. F, page 8) was one inch longer than the overvest, the color and pattern exactly like the blue overvest. Linen or leather trousers were fastened around the knees by ribbons strung through zigzag holes (Fig. F, page 8).

B

D

C

A

Village Sunday Costumes and Saxon Smock

Upper Hessen Maidens' Sunday Costumes

E   F

German Festival Costumes

Village Everyday Dress

Costumes of Thuringia

Costumes of Thuringia

Black Forest Costumes

[2]

The History of Germany

In ancient times the nation we know as Germany today was a part of the Roman Empire. After the conquest of Gaul in 58 B.C., during the reign of Gaius Julius Caesar, the Romans clashed with their northern neighbors. Tribes known as Germani (a Celtic word meaning "the shouters") were subjugated and pursued across the Rhine to their ancestral home known as Germania. Before Roman occupation the Germani tribes' homeland was in Southern Scandinavia, Denmark, and Schleswig-Holstein. The tribes began pushing south and westward in Roman times.

In 9 A.D. Germanic tribes led an uprising against the Romans and were victorious in forcing Roman withdrawal to the west bank of the Rhine River. Cities known as Cologne, Augsburg, Trier, and Bonn were established in Germania during that period.

The Germanic tribes, once seminomadic, began to federate into nations: Alamanni, Burgundians, Franks, Frisii, Goths, Lombards, Saxons, Suevi, Vandals. In the third and fourth centuries Roman emperors experienced internal and foreign problems and allowed the Germanic groupings as allies to settle within the imperial domain. Roman power declined in the fifth century and Germanic tribes overran large portions of Roman territory including Gaul. Clovis I, leader of the Franks, became master of Gaul and a large part east of the Rhine known as the Frankish Empire (most of present-day France and Germany).

The terms of the Treaty of Verdun after the death of Charlemagne in 814 A.D. divided his empire among his grandsons. Louis II received the east portion, now modern Germany. The west portion, now modern France, was separated from the east by an intermediate kingdom which disintegrated into various principalities becoming the source of friction for centuries between east and west. Feudatory chieftains of the duchies of Saxony, Swabia and Bavaria retained absolute control of their domains and elected sovereigns.

The first ruler of significance in Germany was Henry I, Duke of Saxony in 919. Henry extended his authority over Swabia and Bavaria creating the first united Germany. The reign of Henry's son Otto I further consolidated Germany by suppressing feudal rebellions, conquering Bohemia, and annexing the Danes. In order to lessen the threat of feudal usurpation Otto I enlisted the prestige and power of the Roman Catholic Church on the side of the crown. He subdivided duchies into smaller units and awarded them to Church dignitaries. In 961 Otto's friendliness to Rome resulted in his invasion of Italy at the request of Pope John XII. In 962 Otto I was awarded for his services an Imperial crown and title by Pope John XII reviving the imperial structure bestowed in 800 A.D. on Charlemagne, Emperor of the Romans. This union was called the Holy Roman Empire.

Germany became a multiplicity of independent or semi-independent states for most of her two-thousand-year history, and was populated with inhabitants of common racial background and language, mutual customs, institutions, and religion. Attempts at statehood in the Middle Ages were incapable of withstanding the effects of feudalism. The German nation disintegrated into numerous principalities followed by political chaos and the expansion or contraction of states following foreign wars and ecclesiastical developments on the continent of Europe. Widespread hostility developed toward tax levies for support of Church hierarchy, clerical corruption and immorality, and papal resistance to taxation of Church property. English theologian John Wycliffe translated this growing resentment against the doctrine and practices of the Church. Bohemian theologian John Huss, influenced by Wycliffe's teachings, started an offensive in central Europe, and was condemned as a heretic and burned at the stake in 1415. His followers kept Germany in turmoil from 1419 to 1434.

In the middle of the fifteenth century Johann Gutenberg of Mainz, Germany, perfected printing a Bible and made it available to the laity. This resulted in a growing number of German scholars and a spirit of inquiry apart from the Vatican in Rome. In 1517, German monk and educator Martin Luther joined the fight against papal policy by posting 95 theses criticizing the selling of papal indulgences on the door of the Wittenburg church. Luther's action precipitated a crisis known as The Reformation. Opulent Church properties were confiscated, and a Protestant movement developed rapidly in Saxony, Hessen, Mecklenburg, and Brandenburg.

In 1552, Protestant Prince Maurice, Duke of Saxony, joined Henry II of France in a series of surprise attacks that were victorious and came to terms with rebellious princes forcing the granting of German Protestant states freedom of worship. The Roman Catholic Church formally sanctioned Lutheranism in the 1555 Peace Treaty of Augsburg. However, a Roman Catholic counter-offensive known as the Counter-Reformation launched a political rivalry between the Holy Roman emperors and the German princes which increased the economic misery in the German countryside.

In 1618 a Bohemian Protestant revolt against religious, political, and social tensions exploded into the Thirty Years' War. All the

Protestant and Catholic states of Germany were involved as were most of the countries of western Europe. It began as a religious war and turned into a fight between France and the Holy Roman Empire for political authority in Europe. The Thirty Years' War damaged the economy of Germany and stopped the movement for national statehood through the Treaty of Westphalia.

In 1701 the Kingdom of Prussia was constituted with King Frederick I, son of Frederick William. Prussia joined Austria and Great Britain in a coalition challenging French supremacy. The military and economic strength of Prussia grew until the 1740 reign of Frederick the Great when the Prussian army invaded Silesia and started a struggle with Austria for control of Germany that resulted in the Seven Years' War from 1756 to 1763.

Then the Napoleonic Wars erupted. Prussia was involved in phases of the wars and events that brought the downfall of Napoleon. Nationalism gained among the German people, but rivalry between Prussia and Austria caused dangerous crises until the accession of William I in 1861. When Otto von Bismarck came to power, domestic and foreign policies were formed that made Prussia the dominant force in the consolidation of Germany. In 1866 Hessen-Kassel was annexed by Prussia. Germany was divided for more than four centuries by religion and until 1871 by numerous political states. In 1871, the German states were welded into a unified nation with a heritage containing a powerful feudatory class, and Prussian monarch William I was proclaimed Emperor of Germany.

The German Empire known as The Reich was made up of a total area of 209,000 square miles with a population of approximately 41,000,000 in 25 states, 13 duchies and principalities, 5 grand duchies, 4 kingdoms, 3 free cities, and some territory gained from France. After The Reich unification, the German Industrial Revolution expanded rapidly. The steel industry, shipbuilding, railway equipment and manufacturing activity moved ahead of other European nations in foreign markets. Industrial growth in Germany provided a base for imperial militarism, and war became a tradition in the German national culture.

Between 1879 and 1882 Germany, Austria-Hungary and Italy formalized a series of secret treaties. William II ascended the German throne in 1888. Bismarck was dismissed in 1890 and imperial colonial policy became increasingly aggressive. A steady deterioration of diplomatic relations between Germany and Great Britain arose with colonial, commercial, and naval rivalries.

On June 28, 1914 a Serbian terrorist assassinated Grand Duke Ferdinand, heir presumptive to the Austro-Hungarian throne. The assassination set off violent reactions among European nations resulting in World War I. The German people entered the conflict fighting on two fronts with patriotism and enthusiasm. There were numerous successes during the initial campaigns, but after the winter of 1914-15 an Allied blockade of ports stopped the flow of raw materials and food into Germany. The entry of the United States into the war April 6, 1917 on the side of the Allies defeated Germany and forced the signing of an armistice on November 11, 1918. The Treaty of Versailles, signed on June 23, 1919, gave Germany full responsibility for the war and imposed reprisals, including the loss of colonial possessions, cession of Alsace-Lorraine to France. It also ceded the coal fields of Saar to France, separated East Prussia from Germany, gave North Schleswig to Denmark, established Danzig as a free city, and imposed restrictions on the German military establishment.

The Weimar Republic, formed at the national assembly in 1919, endured for about a year. There was bitter economic and political chaos in Germany. Inflation bankrupted large sections of the population. A group of extreme nationalists met November 8, 1923 under the leadership of Adolph Hitler and attempted a coup d'etat at Munich known as the "Beer Hall Putsch" which was quelled. Hitler was imprisoned for less than a year of his five-year term, and then he resumed leadership of the German nationalists later known as the National Socialist (Nazi) Party.

A world economic crisis began in late 1929 with repercussions in Germany. By the end of 1931 there were over 6,000,000 Germans unemployed. An organized military strong-arm squad known as the Storm Troops of the Nazi Party campaigned against the Communists and their supporters. Martial law in Berlin and parts of Prussia removed numerous Social Democratic government officials from office. Continuing disunity of political parties prevailed, but President Hindenburg refused on January 28, 1933 to dissolve the Reichstag and hold new elections. The cabinet fell the same day and two days later Hindenburg commissioned Adolph Hitler to form a new government. The Nazi caucus gained passage of legislation granting Hitler broad dictatorial powers. Reichstag action ended the Weimar Republic and established the Third Reich. All evidence of German Democratic, Nationalist and opposition political parties was eradicated.

When President Hindenburg died in 1934, Hitler claimed the title of Führer and the Nazi regime took over every aspect of German life. National Socialism dominated Germany and Europe. At the Geneva Disarmament Conference on April 25, 1933, the Third Reich rejected the arms limitations provisions of the Treaty of Versailles. Arms production escalated in Germany, ending unemployment and restoring the German economy.

The Nazi pursuit of Germany's ancient past through archaeology under the leadership of Heinrich Himmler established the locations of several ancient Germanic tribe sites in Eastern Europe, giving rise to a Nazi invasion to reclaim those lands for Germany.

Italy invaded Ethiopia in 1935, and the diplomacy of the Third Reich and Italy began parallel movements. In 1938 Austria submitted to German demands and became a state of the Third Reich. Italy completed a military alliance with Germany in May 1939. French and British governments began negotiations with the U.S.S.R. to find an acceptable method for joint action against further Nazi aggression. In August 1939 the U.S.S.R. and Germany completed a non-aggression trade pact. The Third Reich was then free to deal with Poland, which it invaded on September 1, 1939.

On September 3, 1939, Great Britain and France declared war on Germany. It was the beginning of World War II. By the spring of 1941, Nazi Germany had subjugated Denmark, Poland, Norway, the Netherlands, Belgium, Luxemburg, France, Yugoslavia and Greece. German and Italian armies in North Africa threatened the Suez Canal. Britain was severely defeated at Dunkirk, and German air raids threatened London. The Soviet Union's seizure of Romanian territory led King Carol of Romania to place his country under the protection of the Third Reich. In May 1941, Rudolph Hess, Deputy Führer of the Third Reich, parachuted into England in an attempt to negotiate a peace settlement. Acting on his own authority he was captured and held as a prisoner of war.

Japan entered the war on the side of Germany and Italy on December 7, 1941 and bombed Pearl Harbor, Hawaii. The United States and Great Britain declared war against Japan the following day. The United States declared war against Germany and Italy on December 11, 1941.

In February 1943 the Russian army strengthened by Lend-Lease supplies from the United States crushed an entire German army at Stalingrad. The Nazis became desperate following reverses inflicted by Anglo-American forces in North Africa. Allied victories and the Anglo-American invasion of Normandy on June 6, 1944 halted the German military forces. A Nazi attempt to assassinate Hitler on July 20, 1944 failed.

The liberation of France and surrender of Romania culminated in a conference of the heads of the United States, Britain, and Soviet governments at Yalta February 1945. Plans were drafted for the unconditional surrender of the Third Reich including occupation of Germany during the postwar period. The United States Army crossed the Rhine on March 8, 1945 in the final phase of the Allied campaign. On April 20, 1945 the Soviet army sieged Berlin. The German capital city fell to the Russians on May 2, 1945. On May 7, 1945, Nazi chief of staff General Alfred Jodl signed the surrender document. The Allied powers controlled the Third Reich beginning on

June 5, 1945. Germany was divided into four zones of occupation: a British zone in the northwest, a Soviet zone in the east, an American zone in the southwest, and a French zone in the west. The future of Germany was debated in the spring of 1947 when the Council of Foreign Ministers met in Moscow. It was impossible to reach any agreement on basic issues. Another session of the council held in London in the autumn of 1947, failed to resolve the disagreements with the Soviet Union, known from then on as the "cold war".

Occupation Zones of Germany:

France - parts of Prussia, Baden, Hessen, Württemberg, and all of Saarland - total area: 16,139 sq.m.

Great Britain - Hamburg and portions of Prussia, Brunswick, Oldenburg, Schaumburg-Lippe, and Lippe - total area: 37,723 sq.m.

Union of Soviet Socialist Republic - Saxony, Thuringia, Mecklenburg, Anhalt, portions of Prussia - total area: 41,623 sq.m.

United States of America - Bavaria, Bremen and parts of Prussia, Baden, Württemberg, and Hessen - total area: 41,506 sq.m.

Russia began blockading Berlin in 1948 when efforts to solve a problem of currency reform failed. Hostility of East Germany toward the West German government's moves toward unity with western powers surfaced in the form of construction of a barbed-wire fence along the East-West boundary, and the installation of a defense army.

Konrad Adenauer of the Christian Democratic Party was elected Chancellor of West Germany in 1953. The next largest political party in the Bundestag was the Social Democrats. A 1954 meeting of the Council of Foreign Ministers in Berlin again failed to agree on German reunification and a treaty with Austria. The West German economy grew by 1955 to be second among Western powers in steel production.

In 1961 the Soviet Union put pressure on the Western powers to conclude peace with East Germany. Physical barriers between East and West German territory were reinforced, including construction of a wall in Berlin that closed the city boundaries, which made it difficult for East Germans to escape to West Germany.

On October 16, 1962 Ludwig Erhard became Chancellor of West Germany when Adenauer resigned. The Free Democratic Party withdrew from the government coalition in 1966 forcing Erhard to resign. Kurt Kiesinger of the Christian Democratic Union became Chancellor when his party formed a coalition with the Social Democratic Party. Socialist leader Willy Brandt, mayor of West Berlin, succeeded Kiesinger as Chancellor after the national election in September 1969.

The domestic and foreign policy of East Germany strictly followed Communist lines. Iraq was the first non-communist nation to recognize East Germany in 1969. The "cold war" between the Soviet Union and Western powers continued to fester until discontent with East Germany's political and economic difficulties spawned an underground organization of East Germans meeting secretly in churches to organize the revolt of November 9, 1989. The Berlin Wall was torn down at the Brandenburg Gate in the heart of the city.

On October 3, 1990, the reunification of East and West Germany was achieved, ending the physical division that existed in the post-World War II era.

THE CITIES OF GERMANY

BERLIN - Capital of Germany, approximately 163 miles southeast of Hamburg, 300 miles west of Warsaw, Poland. Located 100 feet above sea level, it is larger than Paris, contains three lakes and several beaches (some for nude bathing), Tegelersee on the northwest, Muggelsee on the southeast, and Wannsee on the southwest; and two rivers -- the Spree and the Oder. Berlin was founded in 1244 A.D. It prospered commercially as a member of the Hanseatic League in the fourteenth century. The city lost its independence in the fifteenth century to Margrave Frederick II of Brandenburg, of the house of Hohenzollern. Berlin's economy declined during the Thirty Years' War until Elector Frederick William in 1640 built a canal connecting the Oder and Spree Rivers and encouraged Protestant refugees from France to emigrate to the city.

In 1709 King Frederick I of Prussia (formerly Frederick III of Brandenburg) merged sections of the city into a capital. King Frederick II built the State Opera and Tiergarten public park. During the Seven Years' War the Austrians and Russians captured Berlin. In 1806 the French under Emperor Napoleon I occupied Berlin and defeated Prussia. German nationalism grew after the overthrow of Napoleon in 1815. Berlin then rivaled Vienna as a center of German culture and in 1871 it became the capital of the new German Empire. It was center of political and social unrest following World War I. The city achieved fame in literature, art and science. Before World War II it became a financial, commercial, industrial and transportation center manufacturing electrical equipment, machinery, steel and iron, locomotives, clothing, packaged foods, pharmaceuticals, precision instruments, musical instruments, printed matter and textiles. The city was an inland port with canals connecting the Elbe River, the North Sea, the Oder River, and the Baltic Sea. After World War II the canals were unimportant as inland waterways. Heavily bombed in air raids during the war, sixty percent of Berlin was totally destroyed before Germany surrendered.

Berlin's nineteenth-century ornamental Prussian style architecture was destroyed in World War II. The horseshoe-shaped castle, Charlottenburg Palace, is the only remaining Hohenzollern Palace in Berlin, surrounded by an expansive garden along the Spree River. The east wing was built by Frederick the Great and the theatre was built by Frederick Wilhelm II. The Egyptian Museum, opposite Charlottenburg Palace, contains the famous Nefertiti artifact from Egypt. The World War II bombed shard of Kaiser Wilhelm Memorial Church has been preserved as a ruin with a plaque, "...to remind us of God's punishment." Beside it is the new church.

In Berlin there is sailing, skiing, Wagnerian opera, earthy cabaret, the restored 1936 Olympic Stadium, Technical University, International Congress Center, Brandenburg Gate, Reichstag Building, Congress Hall, Bellevue Palace, Victory Column, Tiergarten Park, Zoo, Friedrichstadt Palace, Humboldt University, German State Opera House, Museum of German History, Folklore Museum, Ethnological Museum, National Galleries, Planetariums, Observatories, Alexander Square, City Hall, Berliner Dom Cathedral, German Theatre, and KaDaWe, the continent's largest department store. Best-known Berlin streets are Kurfurstendamm and Unter der Linden, a wide boulevard lined with Linden trees.

BREMEN - Capital city of the State of Bremen, located on both banks of the Weser River, 46 miles from the North Sea. It is divided into an old town and a new town. A Hanseatic and medieval city, it features a twelfth-century Romanesque St. Peter Cathedral, fifteenth-century Gothic Rathaus, and seventeenth-century Merchants' Hall. Shipbuilding has been the chief industry.

Bremen was a missionary center during the campaigns of Frankish emperor Charlemagne to Christianize the pagans of north Germany. Under 450 years of clerical rule it became a leading commercial city. The mercantile class won political control in 1433 A.D. In 1532 the city joined an alliance against the Holy Roman Empire. At the end of the Thirty Years' War in 1648 Bremen became a Swedish possession and revolted against Swedish rule in 1666. Complete independence was won by 1741. In 1806 Bremen was seized by the French in the Napoleonic Wars. At end of the wars Bremen was made a free state in the 1815 Treaty of Vienna.

Bremen was heavily bombed by Allied forces during World War II.

BREMERHAVEN - Seaport of State of Bremen founded in 1827, 10 miles from the North Sea and about 38 miles northeast of the city of Bremen. Large harbor and many docks. Shipbuilding, shipping and fishing center. In the mid-19th century large numbers of emigrants sailed from this port for North America. After World War II Bremerhaven was the shipping terminal for U.S. occupation forces in Germany.

COLOGNE - North-Rhine Westphalia city located on the Rhine River, 325 miles southwest of Berlin. Originally it was the village of the Ubii, a Germanic tribe. The history of Cologne begins around 50 B.C. when Gaius Julius Caesar extended the borders of the Roman Empire as far as the Rhine and formed an alliance with the Ubii. Around 38 B.C. Marcus Agrippa (son-in-law of Emperor Augustus) founded the "city of Ubii". The Ubii Monument, the oldest squared stone masonry structure ever found north of the Alps (4/5 B.C.), dates from the period before Cologne became "Colonia" in 50 A.D. Empress Julia Agrippa was born and brought up in Cologne and the city was named after her. Medieval Cologne was a crescent-shaped enclosure with ramparts, walls and gates.

During the French Revolution, Cologne was seized and annexed to France. After the defeat of Napoleon the Congress of Vienna in 1815 assigned Cologne to Prussia. The British bombed Cologne in World War I and the city became the headquarters for the British occupation army from 1918 to 1926. The Gothic cathedral in the heart of the city, begun in 1248 and completed in 1880, has excavations uncovering the remains of a Roman pagan temple and traces of an early Christian church which probably extended into the sixth century. The great bell in the south tower was cast in 1874 from French cannon captured in the Franco-Prussian War and is one of largest in the world. The cathedral is the site of the Shrine of the Magi, completed in 1220 A.D. A gold sarcophagus holds the sacred bones of the three Magi, object of many pilgrimages. The cathedral was slightly damaged by Allied forces air raids in World War II. Target of frequent air raids, the old town containing some Roman and medieval parts of the city was ninety percent destroyed. The Hansa Saal, where the first meeting of the Hanseatic League was held in 1366, has been restored. Cologne was in the British occupation zone after the defeat of Germany in 1945.

DRESDEN - Capital of State of Saxony, commercial and industrial city about 100 miles south of Berlin on the banks of the Elbe River. Founded in the twelfth century, it was the seat of government of

Henry, Margrave of Meissen. When he died in 1288, Wenceslaus II of Bohemia controlled the city. The Margrave of Meissen regained control in the fourteenth century from the Margrave of Brandenburg. Albert III, Duke of Saxony, made Dresden the capital of his domain in 1485. The city suffered severe damage during the Seven Years' War and the Napoleonic Wars. Napoleon's 1813 headquarters were in Dresden.

The second half of the nineteenth century brought an expansion of Dresden. British and American air raids seriously damaged the city in 1945. About one-third of Dresden's Baroque Age masterpieces of architecture survived the bombs. The Soviet Union captured Dresden in May 1945 and it remained in the Soviet occupation zone.

Many bridges connect the divisions of the city. Dresden is known for its churches. The Frauenkirche, built 1726 to 1743, in bombed ruins preserved since February 1945 suggests that it was the greatest Baroque church in Dresden. After the reunification of Germany in 1990, reconstruction of the church began. The palatial Zwinger museum, completed between 1711 and 1732 is an architectural Rococo extravaganza which was reconstructed after World War II. It contains a picture gallery of 2,500 paintings of masters of Italian, Flemish and Dutch schools, and 350,000 engravings, drawings, and zoological, mineralogical, and scientific exhibits. The Johanneum Museum has a collection of porcelain from all parts of the world. Dresden porcelain is manufactured at Meissen, about 15 miles northwest of the city.

DUSSELDORF- City of castle residences of counts and dukes of Berg. Originated in 1288 A.D. It is the capital of the state of North Rhine-Westphalia, located on the Rhine River near industrial cities in the Ruhr. Dusseldorf has been damaged many times by war. It was the capital of the Napoleonic grand duchy of Berg in 1805,and became a part of Prussia in 1815. After 1870 it was the industrial center in Ruhr, manufacturing metal products, machinery, tools, chemicals, dyes, paper products, textiles, technical and scientific instruments, musical instruments, furniture, glass, porcelain, enamel, cement, beer, printing and publishing. Allied forces occupied the city after World War I from 1921 to 1925. After World War II Dusseldorf was in the British zone of occupation.

FRANKFURT - Probably established in the first century A.D. on the north bank of the Main River, about 22 miles east of its confluence with the Rhine at Mainz. During the reign of Charlemagne several imperial councils were held in Frankfurt. It became an independent city in 1220 and was declared a free city in 1245. Inhabitants of Frankfurt adopted the Protestant religion about 1520 and it became a stronghold of Protestantism. Frankfurt lost its independence when the Confederation of the Rhine was formed in 1806, but regained free city status in 1815. The city was seized by the Prussians in 1866 during the Seven Weeks' War between Austria and Prussia. Much of Frankfurt was destroyed in World War II by Allied bombing in 1944. In March 1945 the U.S. Army captured Frankfurt. Frankfurt is the largest commercial and industrial city of the State of Hesse in the center of Germany. The Frankfurt main railway station is the largest train station in Europe. The Old Opera Theater reopened in 1981 after war damage repair. *Stufengiebel* architecture (see glossary) can be seen in the historic area. The Goethe Museum - Goethe's birthplace was completely destroyed in World War II and rebuilt 1946-51; original contents were stored and can now be viewed again.

HAMBURG - Capital of the State of Hamburg, principal seaport and second-largest city of Germany, located on the north branch of the Elbe River about 75 miles inland from the North Sea. It was originally a fortress of the Frankish emperor Charlemagne. In 808 A.D. it was the center of the Christian effort to convert pagan tribes in northern Europe. It was a member of the Hanseatic League in the thirteenth century and a free city of the Holy Roman Empire in 1510 A.D. The city declined during the Thirty Years' War. In 1806 Napoleon's army occupied Hamburg. Many Hanseatic buildings burned in "Great Fire" of 1842. It was a member of the North German Confederation from 1866 to 1871 when it became a state of the German Empire. The Hamburg uprising of November 1918, on the eve of the German surrender of World War I, overthrew the German Empire and formed the Weimar Republic.

Hamburg was a World War II submarine base and Nazi center for the war effort. It was a shipbuilding center prior to and during World War II, but was heavily damaged by Allied air raids. British troops occupied the city in May 1945. Industries: food processing, jute spinning, brewing, distilled spirits, soap, furniture, wallpaper, tobacco products, fertilizer, chemicals, motor vehicles, bicycles, sewing machines, precision instruments, machinery, textile products. Five-hundred consulates are located in Hamburg's port areas.

Features of the city are an old section traversed by many canals and bridges, an ancient rampart converted into gardens, public square, Renaissance-style Rathaus, twelfth-century St. Peter Church, medieval St. Catharine and St. Jacob Churches, Renaissance style St. Michael Church (crypts - Carl Philip Emanuel Bach and Johannes Brahms) completed in 1762, Gothic style St. Nicholas Church with 482-foot spire, one of the highest in the world. Music composers Felix Mendelssohn and Johannes Brahms were born in Hamburg.

HANNOVER - Capital of the State of Lower Saxony, and a railway and industrial center about 158 miles west of Berlin. In 1241 A.D. Duke Otto, founder of the house of Luneburg-Brunswick (later named Hannover) granted a municipal charter to Hannover. In 1481 it became a member of the Hanseatic League. Hannover grew slowly. Commercial and industrial development began after annexation to Prussia. Hannover was a target of Allied air raids in World War II and had to be redesigned following the war. The city was captured by U.S. armed forces in April 1945 and later was in the British occupation zone after November 1, 1946. Features of the city: old medieval section; tower of Protestant Marktkirche of St. Georg and St. Jacobus dating from 1300 and a symbol of old Hannover was rebuilt after 1945 according to original plans; Gothic Rathaus dating between 1439 and 1455 restored after World War II; former royal palace from 1640, now a museum of art; Opera House, burnt down in World War II and rebuilt in old classical and Renaissance style; Herrenhausen, the summer residence of the royal family of Hannover.

KASSEL - City of the State of Hesse located on the Fulda River. Originally a Roman colony. Incorporated in the twelfth century into Kingdom of Thuringia. Acquired by the Landgraves of Hessen as a prince's seat in the thirteenth century. French Huguenots settled in Kassel in the seventeenth century. Frederich II of Hessen-Kassel (1760-85) hired out 12,000 of his countrymen as mercenaries to England in the North American War of Independence, to pay for the magnificence of the castles, palaces and parks created in the city by the eighteenth-century Margraves.

Kassel was the capital of the Prussian province of Hessen-Nassau in 1867. The Grimm brothers, Jacob (1785-1863) and Wilhelm (1786-1859), authors of famous fairy tales, were hired as Kassel librarians by the Landgrave of Hessen.

Bombed by Allied forces during air raids of World War II, the Kassel Rathaus and all its records were destroyed. War destruction altered the appearance of the city, from the gargantuan Hercules statue in Wilhelmshöhe Park to Friedrichsplatz and Karlsaue, the symmetrical park & orangery laid out by Landgrave Karl. Features of the city: seventeenth-century gabled houses; palaces; Elisabeth Hospital; fourteenth-century Protestant Bruderkirche; museums; art galleries; and industrial-arts school.

LEIPZIG - Located 111 miles southwest of Berlin and inhabited by Slavic tribes before 1000 A.D. The Margraves of Meissen promoted fairs in Leipzig in the twelfth century. The electors of Saxony granted the right of self-government to Leipzig in the fifteenth century and continued the fairs. During the Thirty Years' War the city was the site of the Battle of Breitenfeld in 1631. The Battle of Leipzig during the Napoleonic Wars took place in 1813. In the eighteenth century Leipzig became a classical literary center. Johann Wolfgang von Goethe and Johann Sebastian Bach studied at the University of Leipzig. The city became one of the musical centers of Europe: Johann Sebastian Bach was the musical director and organist from 1723 to 1750 at Thomaskirche, which was built in the thirteenth century (and now houses Bach's tomb); Felix Mendelssohn conducted concerts in Leipzig from 1835 until his death in 1847; Composer Richard Wagner was born in Leipzig. The New Rathaus is the site where Martin Luther held a debate with Johann Eck in 1519.

For centuries, Leipzig was known principally as the host of trade fairs that attracted buyers and sellers from around the world. This tradition was kept alive in the twentieth-century communist era, and fairs are still held in September and at Easter. Leipzig is also famous for its printing and publishing houses. The German book publishing industry has had its headquarters in Leipzig since 1825, establishing the city as a print media center.

Heavily bombed by Allied forces in World War II, Leipzig was in the Soviet Union zone of occupation. It was on the streets of this historic city that the movement to overthrow German communism gathered force in the autumn of 1989. In 1990 prayer vigils inaugurated at St. Nikolai Church inspired the democracy movement which toppled the Berlin Wall and led to German reunification. Throughout Leipzig, old buildings are restored, new businesses are open, an opera company and symphony orchestra thrive. Of interest: botanical gardens, parks, astronomical observatory, museum, conservatory of music, theater, and vocational schools.

MARBURG - Medieval St. Elisabeth City, seat of the Landgraves of Hessen. The emblem of the city and an important ecclesiastical pilgrimage church is Elisabethkirche, built 1235 A.D. It is the first pure Gothic building in Germany, built over the tomb of Landgravine Elisabeth von Thuringen. The church contains a notable high altar, and the thirteenth-century gold Elisabeth Shrine, made of precious stones and filigree. In the transept of the church are the tombs of the Landgraves of Thuringen-Hessen including Henry I.

The city of Marburg is known for the 1529 Colloquy of Marburg, an attempt to unify the Protestant and Reformed princes. Luther,

Melanchthon, and the Swiss theologian Zwingli were involved in the event.

Of interest: Marburg University, founded in 1527; numerous seventeenth- and eighteenth-century half-timbered buildings; Teutonic Order buildings; thirteenth-century palace seat of the Landgraves of Hessen started by Duchess Sophia, daughter of St. Elisabeth; Rathaus and Marktplatz built in 1512-27; museums - academic collection of 600 copies of Greek and Roman sculpture.

MUNICH - Capital of Bavaria since 1255 A.D., university and cultural center of south Germany. A fire destroyed the city in the fourteenth century. Sweden under Gustavus Adolphus occupied Munich during the Thirty Years' War. The city was the center of European culture under Duke Wilhelm IV, Ludwig I, and Ludwig II, and a center of the arts in the nineteenth century during the reigns of Kings Louis I and Maximilian. The city became a music center under Louis II, patron of composers Richard Wagner and Richard Strauss, both of whom lived in the city. Adolph Hitler's National Socialist German Workers Party (Nazi) began in Munich's Beer Hall Putsch of 1923.

Munich was heavily damaged by bombs during World War II, requiring extensive restoration of major buildings. The city was in the U.S. zone of occupation after 1945.

Landmarks: twin onion-domed Gothic Frauenkirche (Church of Our Lady) restored after World War II; restored Rathaus at Marienplatz; restored Alte Pinakothek and Neue Pinakothek Museums, Deutches Museum, Munchner Stadtmuseum, Bavarian National Museum; National Theater; 1972 Olympic Stadium; King Ludwig II's Nymphenburg Palace; Jesuit Church of St. Michael built in the sixteenth century containing the royal crypts of Wilhelm V, Maximilian I, Ludwig II. The University of Munich was founded in 1472 and moved to the city in 1826. The lithography process was invented in Munich at the end of the eighteenth century.

NURNBERG - Predominantly medieval city of Bavaria owned by German nobles and unaffected by the Baroque or any other period of history. It was first mentioned in documents dated 1050 A.D. It was made a free imperial town in 1219, and became a center of culture and manufacturing in the fifteenth and sixteenth centuries. Fifteenth-century painter and engraver Albrecht Dürer worked in the city. It was annexed to the Kingdom of Bavaria in 1806. In 1933 the National Socialist (Nazi Party) convened in Nurnberg. World War II Allied forces bombed the city heavily. It was the site of the trials of Nazi war criminals and was occupied by U.S. armed forces during the postwar era. Of interest: medieval Gothic churches with fine altars; Albrecht Dürer and Hans Sachs homes; eleventh-century castle; Rathaus; National Museum; Richard Wagner Platz Opera House; Municipal Library.

POTSDAM - Center of history and culture on the Havel River southwest of Berlin. Architectural site of the French Rococo-style Sanssouci Palace built in the middle of the eighteenth century by Frederick the Great, the Hohenzollern ruler who extended Prussian power and paved the way for the 1871 German Empire. Frederick the Great's tomb is in the gardens of the Palace. His father, King Frederick William I is buried in the royal mausoleum at Friedens (Peace) Church in Potsdam. The city was the site of the 1945 Potsdam Conference of heads of state of the U.S.A., Great Britain, and the Soviet Union following the unconditional surrender of the Third Reich in World War II.

STUTTGART - Capital of Baden-Württemberg, located on the Neckar River, 127 miles southeast of Frankfurt. The history of this city dates from 1229. It was the target of Allied forces air raids during World War II. French troops captured the city April 22, 1945. It was known as the center of the German book trade. Cultural features: technical university; agricultural college; academy of music, drama and art; large Württemberg State Library; seat of German Schiller Society; Rathaus; New Palace (1746-1807) with Schlossgarten; Old Palace (sixteenth century); King William column, 93 feet high; statue of Schiller; Gothic Stiftskirche from 1436; Museums of Antiquities and Art; Protestant Collegiate Church of Das Heilige Kreuz contains the sixteenth-century sculptured crypts of the Counts of Württemberg.

WIESBADEN - Capital of the State of Hesse since 1946. Located about 20 miles west of Frankfurt on the Rhine River. In the third century the Celts founded a settlement on the site of this city that was a spa and a fortification of the Romans. The Nassau family possessed the city in the eleventh century, and it became the capital of the Duchy of Nassau 1815-1866 when it became part of the Prussian province of Hessen-Nassau. Most of the city suffered damage during World War II and was captured by American forces in 1945. It was under the U.S. zone of occupation after World War II.

Wiesbaden continues to be an important spa and conference center, transportation and manufacturing city. Of interest: Nassau State Library; former royal residences; Kurhaus; Colonnade; Alte Rathaus; Neus Rathaus; museums; theatres for opera, operetta, musicals, drama, ballet; and remnants of a Roman wall called "heathen's wall."

Important Dates in German History

B.C. Germani tribes migrate from their original homeland in eastern Europe to borders of Roman Empire.

58 B.C. Emperor Gaius Julius Caesar finds Germani tribes in conquest of Gaul.

1 A.D. Roman historian Tacitus writes description of Germans.

9 A.D. Germani tribes victorious over Roman legions.

Early Middle Ages

Fifth Century Decline of Roman power. Frankish Emperor Clovis I invades and rules Gaul.

800 Charlemagne, King of the Franks crowned emperor of the Romans by the Pope. Holy Roman Empire, German-Italian union.

843 Treaty of Verdun decrees the division of the Holy Roman Empire among the three grandsons of Charlemagne.

The Saxon Dynasty

919 Henry, Duke of Saxony obtains throne, unites Germany.

936-973 Reign of Emperor Otto I (the Great), son of Henry I.

973-983 Emperor Otto II, son of Otto I.

983-1002 Emperor Otto III, son of Otto II.

1002-1024 Emperor Henry II, great-grandson of Henry I, second cousin of his immediate predecessor, and last emperor of the Saxon dynasty.

The Salian Dynasty

1024-1039 Emperor Conrad II, descends in female line from Otto the Great, by election.

1039-1056 Emperor Henry III, son of Conrad II.

1056-1106 Emperor Henry IV, son of Henry III.

1076 Confrontation of Henry IV with Pope Gregory VII, civil war until 1122.

1106-1125 Emperor Henry V, son of Henry IV.

1125-1137 Election of Lothair II, Saxon papal partisan, instead of the nephew Henry V designated as his successor, plunges Germany into civil war.

The Hohenstaufen Dynasty

1138-1152 King Conrad II, elected in preference to Lothair's designated heir, Henry the Proud, but never crowned emperor. Losses in the Second Crusade bring economic chaos.

1152-1190 Emperor Frederick I, nephew of Conrad III, restores the German realm.

1190-1197 Emperor Henry VI, period of turmoil in Germany.

1198-1214 Civil War over succession after the untimely death of Henry VI.

1216 Emperor Frederick II challenges the power of the papacy.

The Late Middle Ages

1250-1273 The Great Interregnum, the period from the death of Conrad IV to the election of King Rudolf of the Hapsburg Dynasty, was used by princes to increase their authority.

The Hapsburg Dynasty

1273-1291 Pope Gregory X consented to the election of German King Rudolph I, first king of the Hapsburgs, but he was never crowned emperor.

1292-1298 King Adolf (of Nassau) is elected instead of the designated heir of Rudolf, but is never crowned emperor.

1298-1308 King Albert I, son of Rudolf of Hapsburg, regains the throne for the Hapsburgs but is never crowned emperor.

1308-1313 Emperor Henry VII (of Luxemburg) rivaled the Hapsburgs for power in Bohemia until the two families merged through nuptial diplomacy.

1415 Frederick of Hohenzollern, the Margrave of Brandenburg, begins the five-hundred-year rule of the Hohenzollern dynasty in north Germany.

1434 John Huss, a Bohemian theologian, is burned at the stake for heretical doctrines. Hussites keep Germany in turmoil.

1438-1439 King Albert II of Hapsburg, great-great-grandson of Albert I regains the throne, but is never crowned emperor. Hapsburgs retain the throne until 1806.

1517-55 Protestant Reformation in Germany. Martin Luther's 95 Theses criticizing papal indulgences are nailed on the church door in Wittenberg.

1521 Diet and Edict of Worms, April 16. Luther, a professor at Wittenberg University, refused to recant and on May 14 was secretly taken to Wartburg Castle by Duke Frederick of Saxony, where he translated the New Testament from Greek to German in ten weeks. It was published September 1522.

1530 Diet of Augsburg - "Augsburg Confession" made public.

1563 Council of Trent. Parish priests instructed to keep registers for baptisms and marriages.

Beginning of Counter-Reformation.

1618 Beginning of the Thirty Years' War that destroyed a large number of German churches and their records.

1648 Westphalia Peace Treaty of the Thirty Years' War giving equal rights for Protestant and Catholic churches in Germany.

1685 Johann Sebastian Bach and George Frederich Handel born.

1648-1721 German Empire in Decay; Austro-Prussian Conflicts.

1756-1763 Seven Years' War

1789-1814 French Revolution and Napoleonic Wars sweep across Europe.

The Nineteenth Century

1797-1840 King Frederick William III, son of Frederick William II.

1806 Holy Roman Empire is dissolved by German-Austrian kings.

1814-1815 Congress in Vienna. The German Federation of 39 States under presidency of Austria is established.

1815-1866 The German Federation.

1867 North German Confederation politically dominated by Prussia following Austro-Prussian War.

1870-1871 Franco-Prussian War caused by candidacy of Hohenzollern prince for Spanish throne, results in fall of French Empire and establishment by Bismarck of German Empire at Versailles.

1888 Kaiser Wilhelm II reign, son of Frederick III.

1890 November 9 dismissal of Bismarck by Kaiser Wilhelm II

The Twentieth Century

1914-1918 World War I: Defeat of Germany and the German monarchy.

1918 November 9, Kaiser Wilhelm II abdication ends rule of Hohenzollern dynasty in face of armed revolution and marked beginning of Germany's turbulent experiment with democracy.

1919 Weimar Constitution, submission to Treaty of Versailles.

1919 The German Republic. Field Marshal Paul von Hindenburg is elected President of the Weimar Republic.

1923 November 9, Adolf Hitler mounted the abortive "Beer Hall Putsch," named himself chancellor, and tried to overthrow the elected government. His arrest gave him an aura of martyrdom that helped in his march to power.

1933 Beginning of The Third Reich.

1938 November 9, *Kristallnacht*, Nazis kill and arrest Jews, burn synagogues and Jewish-owned businesses. Shattered glass littered the streets on the morning of the 9th.
German occupation of Austria.

1939-1945 World War II: defeat of Germany.

1948 April 1, British, French, and American zones become single state. Berlin Blockade begun by Russia. Berlin airlift begins.

1949 September 30, Berlin Blockade lifted.

1949 Federal Republic of Germany - American, British, and French zones of occupation.
German Democratic Republic - Soviet zone of occupation.

1961 Wall erected between East and West Berlin.

1989 November 9 Revolution in East Germany - Berlin Wall comes down, signaling end of the Cold War.

1990 October 3 Reunification of East Germany & West Germany. End of the postwar era.

[3]

How to Begin to Trace Your German Ancestry

Millions of Germans have emigrated from the Old Country since colonial days in America. The peak period of immigration in the United States was the eighty years between 1820 and 1900. The German pioneers of North America left all sorts of tracks for family-tree detectives to follow.

Much research has already been done and is available to the public through many sources, making it easier today to begin searching for German roots. Before beginning to search for German roots it is important to realize that German-speaking immigrants from other countries of Europe were often identified as "Germans" even though they were not from Germany, which could lead a genealogy search to Austria, Switzerland, Poland or other countries.

German-descendant sleuths must do their homework thoroughly to search family history or pay a genealogist to do it. Relatives' stories and heirlooms enrich family history, but it takes legal documents and official records to prove family genealogy. Documenting a family tree means nailing down vital statistics such as births, marriages, divorces, and deaths.

Genealogy work involves compiling the history of an individual family, therefore, it is important to develop the habit of recording places and sources where the documentation of each generation is found. This is valuable information for later reference of family members at a future date when proof is needed to qualify for government papers, medical history, or membership in organizations based on hereditary identity.

Tracing family roots means starting with present-day information and searching backwards in time. Do not mislead your research by starting with people of the same surname that you would like to connect with your family and attempting to trace them down to you. Everyone with the same surname is not related to you. Many immigrants from Germany in the seventeenth, eighteenth, and nineteenth centuries "Americanized" the spelling of their names at the time of their immigration or early in their family life in the New World.

Many German immigrants were illiterate, could not read or write their own name, and signed documents with an X. Surnames became distorted due to the dialects spoken by immigrants, and the English-speaking officials spelled names phonetically to record what they heard. Often several documents researched on the same person show different surname spellings due to the name sounding different to each official filling out the documents at different times. Research may show a surname spelled differently in the same document. In my family the name Möller was changed to Moeller. A will from another branch of my family dated 1826 spelled the surname two different ways -- Bryner and Briner.

To accomplish successful genealogy research it is important and well worth your time to study the history of all localities where your German relatives lived in the United States. Besides American Indians, other populations probably lived in the vicinity of your research before the immigration of your German ancestors. This may have had an impact on your immigrant or pioneer ancestors. For example, in Oregon many French-Canadians, most of whom were former employees of the Hudson's Bay Company, settled in the area known as French Prairie in Marion County, Oregon before the wagon trains of early settlers arrived to populate the land. Their influence and existence in the area had a profound impact on early pioneers arriving in wagon trains.

The more that is understood about the area in which progenitors and ascendants lived, the more accurate your genealogy research will be. Background knowledge of local history prevents errors from creeping into family history because it is possible to quickly identify pieces of the generation puzzle that do not fit. The history of a locality can also give clues to intentionally or otherwise lost-over-time information about a family, for example, a pioneer relative married to a Native American.

If you are just beginning to work on your German family tree, the first determination that must be made is whether anyone else in your family has previously searched family genealogy. Ask the older generation of your family and they will probably know if any relative has been interested in genealogy. (See illustration of German-American family genealogy in German language, page 35.) If anyone in your family has gathered information about births and deaths, you must carefully evaluate the accuracy and source of that information. Such records are usually collected from memory over potluck meals at a reunion without the benefit of documents to look at, and as a result many records are slightly inaccurate and contain errors. There is no substitute for checking out primary sources to verify records. Before proceeding further, check with the nearest LDS (Mormon Church) branch library to see if someone has already traced your family line.

If detective work reveals that no genealogy searches have been made in your family, then you must start from scratch and decide whether to trace roots of the surname of the male line or the female

```
         "    -    Happel Familie . - "
Katharina Elisabeth ,Tochter v Adam Werning u dessen Ehefrau Jeanette,eine
   Tochter v Anton Brehm u. dessen Ehefr.Kathar.geb.Pfaffenbach
   geb.am 24.Jan.1855 in Dankerode,Kreiss Rothenburg a der Fulda,
   Provinz Hessen-Nassau,Deutschland.Mit ihren Eltern kam sie im
   Jahre 1870 nach America;und zwar nach Eldorado Twp.,Benton CO.
   Iowa.AM 3.Juli 1874 trat sie in den heiligen Eheestand mit :
Peter Happel,Sohn des Herren Andreas Happel u dessenEhefr.  geb ....
   geb.am4.Maerz 1851 in Altenheina,Kreiss Frankenberg,Provinz
   Hessen-Nassau,Deutschland.Im Jahre 1864 kam er rit seinen Eltern
   nach America und liess n sich in Fremont Tw .Benten Co.,Iowa ;
   nieder ;wo er sich dann auch Land erwarb und verheiratet hat.
   Spaeter zog die Familie in die Gegend nord v New Hall .
   Deren Kinder sind :
```

```
        1.Anreas Adam    geb. den 25.Sept.1875   in Fremont Twp.
        2.Christine        ''     '' 13.Fehr.1877    ''    ''    ''
        3.Elisabeth        ''     '' 27.Dec. 1878    ''    ''    ''
        4.Heinrich         ''     ''  4.Febr.1881    ''    ''    ''
        5.Katharina        ''     ''11.Jan. 1883   ''Eldorado ''
        6.August           ''     ''  1.April1885    ''    ''    ''
        7.Wilhelm          ''     '' 29.Jan. 1388    ''    ''    ''
        8.Maria            ''     '' 26.Dec. 1890    ''    ''    ''
        9.Andeas           ''     ''  3.Juni 1893    ''    ''    ''
       10.Anna             ''     '' 22.Okt. 1895    ''    ''    ''
```

```
        Der Vater starb am 13.MAI 1902 und wurde auf dem Gottesacks
     der Stephanus Gem.bei Atkins ,christlich beerdigt.
     Die Mutter wohnt seid April 1906 in Van Horn .
1.Adam ,verehlichte sich am 25.Febr.1902 mit Kathar.,Tochter des Herren
     Christ.Rinderknecht u Ehefrau Anna geb Nell,geb.a 24.Febr.'82,
                                              nahe Van Horn .
     Deren Kinder,auf ihrem Landgut nahe Vinton,geboren :
        a.Jeanette am    24.Maerz  1903 .
        B.Alfred   ''    17. Dec.  1904.
        c.Gertrud  ''    19. Dec.  1905 .
        d.Lore     ''     6. Juni  1906 .
        e.
2.Christine,verehl. sich am 9.Maerz1893 mit Heinrich Krug,Sohn des Herren
     Johann Krug u Ehefrau     geb.
                             geb. am  9.Febr.1873 in Fremont Twp .
     Deren Kinder,auf den Landgut nahe Atkins in Linn Co.),geboren :
        a./Arthur &Emma (Zwillinge) am27.Sept. 1899.
        b. Clarence             '' 6.Sept. 1901.
        c. Walter               '' 2.Aug.  1904.
        d. Gerhard              '' 25.April 1909.
        e.
3.Elisabeth,verehl.sich am 18.Febr.1903 mit August Krug,Sohn v(siehe oben)
                           geb.am 16.Febr.1874 in Fremont Twp,Ia
     Deren Kinder,auf dem Landgut nahe Atkins,Benton Co.,geboren :
        a.Edna        10.Mai  1904 .
        b.Harvey      22.Juli 1906 .
        c.Ilma        15.Juni 1908 .
        d.Irene        3.Sept.1910.
```

German Language Genealogy of German-American Family

line. You may wish, eventually, to trace both sides of your family, but caution should be taken to not undertake too many surname searches at the same time. However, German pioneer families often married other families that immigrated from the same village in Germany. This causes an exception to the aboved-mentioned warning and creates a need to search both the male and female family surnames simultaneously, thus saving time, energy and money in the process of verifying clues. Follow these steps:

1. Start with yourself and your parents. Write down everything you know about your family. Talk with your parents about it. Don't rely on memory. Work back in time. Dates, names and places are vital information. Record full names (Christian first name, middle name or names, surname), birth date and location, marriage(s) date and location, date of death and location, burial location, and as much other information as your family can provide. It's usually not difficult when you begin with yourself and your parents. Records and clues abound around your home. Gather together information from the closet, the attic, the garage, from under the bed, anywhere you may have stashed things away. Include what you find in old trunks (See illustration on page 37, trunk of Johann Justus Krug which was made in Löhlbach, Germany and brought to America in 1864), desk and bureau drawers full of old letters, newspaper clippings, birth and marriage certificates and announcements, military records, occupational records, pensions, diaries and journals, photo albums (See illustration page iv, immigrants Peter Johann Happel and Katharina Elisabeth Werning), scrapbooks, school records and yearbooks, fraternal awards, legal papers (wills, deeds, guardianship), report cards, diplomas, passports, financial records, checkbook stubs, Bible records, souvenirs and mementos.

When recording dates, develop the habit of listing the day first, the month second, the year last, for example, a person born May 14, 1931 is recorded 14 May 1931. All reliable genealogical records are kept in this form to prevent mistakes and confusion in reading days and months when making accurate genealogical records. The separation of the numbers of the day and year makes it possible to detect inconsistencies in records when the year does not correspond to the generation. When written all in number form, for example, 14/5/31 could not be the fourteenth month.

Do not simply record only the date of birth, marriage and death. Include place of birth, place of marriage(s), place of death, location of burial cemeteries. This kind of record begins to formulate a historical story about your family as the record grows that may save years of time and expense in research.

2. Start a list of all living relatives and their addresses. Also record names and addresses, if known, of neighbors and friends

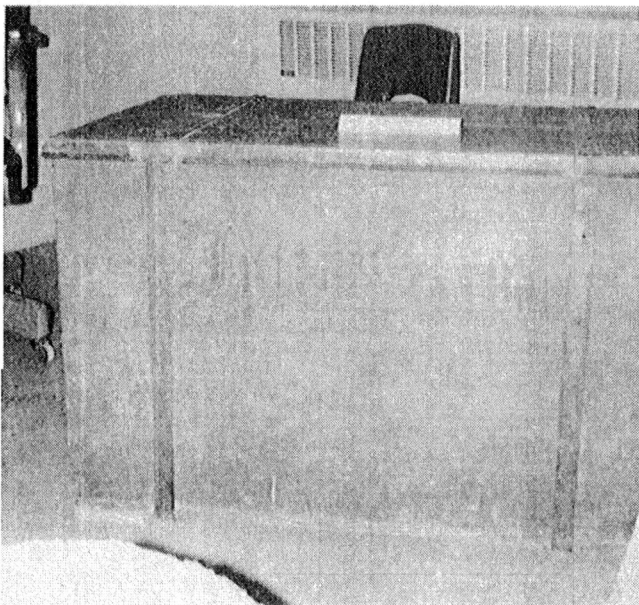

JUSTUS KRUG

Trunk made in Löhlbach, Germany, brought to America in 1865
by immigrant Johann Justus Krug.

of the family that are recalled in searching the family tree with family members. This list can be a valuable resource for future research.

The German culture has developed patrilineally, and the men in the family usually know a great deal of genealogical information about their relatives: where they were born, who they married, when they died, and quite often they know the cause of death. In some German families the youngest generation carries on the Old Country tradition of memorizing the birthdays in the German extended family by playing the Birthday Memory Game, which is passed down from generation to generation at family reunions. All children of the extended family could play the game, no one was left out and no properties were required. I played the game while growing up on a farm in the Midwest and an uncle known for his expert memory monitored the children at play for genealogy accuracy when we competed. The first cousins stood in a circle with the oldest cousin starting the game by reciting from memory in correct birth order, the full name and birth date of each cousin. When a child made a mistake they left the circle and sat down. The more often the game was played the easier it became to remember accurately, therefore, cousins eagerly requested playing the game over and over while waiting for the reunion meal to begin. We caught on quickly that standing in the circle, at the beginning of the game, next to the cousin born closest to one's own birthday made winning easier. Each time the game was played there was a reshuffling of positions in the circle. The result: easier concentration on full names, months, days and years. In the process we developed a close kinship with our nearest cousin in age, forming age-sets in the extended family that often lasted for a lifetime.

The traditional German Birthday Memory Game disappeared with the breakdown of extended family life and the emergence of the smaller, nuclear family. While attending a centennial celebration in my native Midwestern community, many years after the birthday game was discontinued, I learned that none of my first cousins had a written account of the family genealogy, though several cousins who had played the traditional Birthday Memory Game as children still retained an excellent memory of the genealogy of our generation. This was an asset in overcoming the problem of resistance of some family members to divulge information. Usually someone in the family knows who will give out family information and who evades any inquiry which they believe to be an invasion of privacy. Sometimes there is fear that information sought may in some way embarrass or discredit the family.

3. Make an individual working sheet for each family (See Family History Chart, page 39) to record information gathered and handed

down by word of mouth. Document all information you have gathered so you can check back, if necessary, and will know if your information is correct. Keep your work organized and be consistent with the records kept. Identification should be as follows:

    a) NAMES (in full: use maiden names for women)
    b) DATES (list day first, then month, year)
    c) PLACES (birth, marriage, death, burial)
    d) KINSHIP (relationships)

Family History Chart

	Date and place of birth	Residence	Religious affiliation
Your full name (maiden name, if any)			
Father's name	Date and place of birth	Mother's name (maiden name)	Date and place of birth
Education	Date and place of marriage	Spouse's name	

YOUR CHILDREN

Sex	Name	When born where	When married where	Married to	If dead, when and where *buried*
1.					
2.					
3.					
4.					
5.					

FAMILY HISTORY

What do you know about the family surname?

Are there traditional first, middle, or nicknames?

Do you know the name of your immigrant ancestor?

What country did he come from?

When and how did he arrive in this country?

What was his occupation?

Which ancestors served in the military?

Is there a family cemetery?

Do you know anyone in the family working on genealogy?

Does anyone still own old photos, letters, family Bible, etc.?

Oral tradition is useful as a guideline leading to further research. What can be learned from the elders in your family is the quickest way to compile family relationships so that you can begin logging information for a family tree or family chart that shows your ancestry from what is known to the unknown.

WORKING FAMILY SHEET

4. Create a simple family tree or ancestor table with the information you have traced about your immediate family. It is easy to do. A pencil and ruler is all that is needed to draw an outline usable for family genealogy. Start by working from yourself back in time and outward in distance. If you prefer to write out an ancestor table, begin writing a brief paragraph about the oldest known ancestor and proceed vertically downward leaving space between each generation to the current generation at the bottom of the page. Both the family tree and ancestor table grow in detail with addition of data of each generation researched.

FAMILY TREE

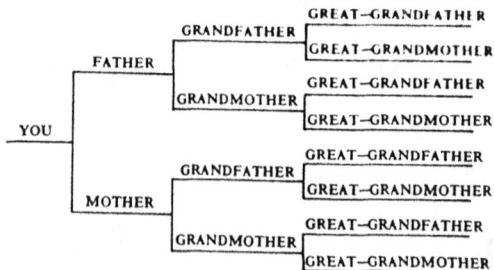

Evaluate what you have traced in your German family line. Oral tradition sometimes contains innocent, and sometimes not so innocent, mistakes. Oral tradition must be verified using primary and secondary sources for accurate genealogical records.

PRIMARY SOURCES

Primary sources are records made by the people involved in the event or occasion; records that provide first-hand evidence are of greater reliability and credibility than secondary sources. Primary sources are mainly local public records including birth, baptism, confirmation, marriage, and death certificates; wills, probate documents, land deeds; church and cemetery records. They are vital in reconstructing family lineage, authenticating information, and providing names of parents and other relations who can be traced to other generations. Often, documents are signed in your ancestor's handwriting, allowing you the opportunity to connect on a personal level with your family of yesteryear.

Usually, primary records can be located in the county (parish in Louisiana) of an ancestor's residence. However, many counties in the United States did not have a sufficient tax base before the twentieth century to establish a County Clerk of Recorder's Office. In those areas, courthouses were not built until well into the twentieth century, however, it is possible to find community records in some states, especially in New England, that go back to earlier centuries when recordings were made by a local clerk. Remember also that primary records are not always totally accurate either. An example of such an error could be a birth certificate inaccurately filled out before a child's name is chosen.

The computer age has led to the centralization of many vital records,and your search may need to be made in a state capital city or designated government office building located away from the area of your ancestor's residence. Check with the local county situation to determine the locality of primary family records. The originals of vital records are in the custody of local, county, or state officials, however, by law you are entitled to obtain copies by paying a fee. Your local library may have an up-to-date pamphlet printed by the U.S. Government Printing Office listing the address, cost and records available in each state and U.S. possession. Most of the records date from the late 1800's.

For more detailed information on searching American public records and court documents, read any of the general genealogical research handbooks on your local or state library genealogy shelves.

Local church records in the United States can verify many vital statistics are usually available upon request. Look for German language baptismal, confirmation, marriage (See illustration on page 42), membership, and cemetery records which include names of spouses, parents, Godparents, and grandparents. Early records in the church and cemetery of the Iowa community of my Krug family also contain a Krog family, and it is important to not confuse the two similar names when identifying cemetery markers or church records.

School records are another primary source to verify birth dates and full names. Parents' signatures may be found on these records.

Oaths of intention and naturalization records are important primary records in tracing German family roots. The local county courthouse, Clerk or Recorder's Office of the ancestor you are searching is the place to look for these records.

246

𝕿𝖗𝖆𝖚-𝕽𝖊𝖌𝖎𝖘𝖙𝖊𝖗

18

No.	Aufgebot.	Trauung.	Namen, Stand und Wohnort des Bräutigams.	Namen und Wohnort der Braut.	Bemerkungen.	Pfarr.

Atkins, Iowa, Parish Marriage Register

[42]

Passports verify birthdate and place, country of birth and citizenship. Old business papers and tax forms show names and evidence of years of residency. Old letters, diaries and military records are primary sources which verify names and give clues to the political, social and religious life of your family. Public libraries and genealogical society libraries have volumes of Federal census records which first began in 1790. Many libraries also have military records beginning with the Revolutionary War. Tracing a family in these records may provide new insights into immigration and residency, size of family, and may make it possible to verify your family through additional earlier generations.

SECONDARY SOURCES

Secondary records sources involve people who were not eyewitnesses to the event or occasion, or those who did not have a primary source to verify information when the record was made. Cemetery inscriptions, obituaries, Bible records, newspaper clippings, and oral reports are examples of secondary sources. Such records are not totally reliable and are only useful when backed up by a primary source. The person who purchased a tombstone usually relied on memory for dates and that memory may not have been accurate, especially if they tried to recall an immigrant's birth when no vital statistics documents were brought from the Old Country. Memories passed down through generations often are inaccurate by at least a year or two.

Americanized names often appear on tombstones of immigrant German ancestors and the names may vary greatly from birth names recorded in Germany. In the villages of my German ancestors in the Old Country it was traditional at baptism to give males the first name of Johann and females the first name of Elisabeth or Katharina. The names were used so repeatedly that when immigrants came to the New World, first names were dropped and second names and nicknames were used as first names. Death notices and tombstone inscriptions continued to use the immigrant's second name as a first name.

In an effort to relate the Old World German heritage to future generations, the graves of my paternal grandmother Happel's family have both headstones and footstones, one inscribed in English and the other in German, together with Bible epitaphs in the German language significant in passing on family values to the next generations.

5. Contact family members, your grandparents, great-aunts and great-uncles by telephone, letter or personal visit to incorporate their information with that which you already have gathered. Many

grandparents and older relatives enjoy talking about the past in their family, and they know names and data about their parents, grandparents, aunts and uncles. They can tell you about family nicknames. German families often had nicknames both in Europe and America. You will learn more about that when you pursue research in Germany. It is important to identify the difference between given names, nicknames and proper names. The older generation are the best source for remembering all names whether full names or nicknames. They often also remember who was named after another relative, or was given the middle name of a relative as was traditional in many German pioneer families.

A discovery in searching full names in German families is that the history of Germany begins to unfold in those family names. For example, the Dukes of Saxony were named Karl, Frederick, August and families in Saxony often named their sons Karl, Frederick, or August. The Dukes of Saxony not only owned the land my relatives lived on in Germany, they also owned the people living on the land and were responsible for protecting them. The German immigrants in my family in the United States continued to name children with these honored names in their family's past history in Germany.

Relatives may own many of the primary and secondary sources you need to trace German ancestry. Once an ancestor is located, look for any other clues that can be found, for example, if a person did something notable, such as serving as a mayor, there is likely to be a newspaper account somewhere that can assist in another further research step. You may get to know your family better, and meet some people you have never known before who will give you the feeling of belonging to an expanded, if not extended, family. Get addresses and write letters to older relatives who live at a distance and correspond with them about your family. Even if you have gathered information by oral tradition from one person in your family, it is important to check out the facts with another older relative even though living at a distance. No doubt some of the information will not be the same. Sometimes the only way to determine exact dates and places when relatives relate different details is to search for documentation of the facts in dispute. At times it may be necessary to check out the data with an older friend of the family who still lives in the community of your family's residence. If it becomes necessary to correspond by mail, keep your requests short, clearly stating exactly what information you are seeking. Type or write a neat letter that can easily be read. It's a good idea to keep a copy of the letter you write, and follow up on your inquiry if you do not receive a reply in a reasonable time.

Do not be surprised if some relatives are uncooperative about supplying the information you are seeking. Do not be discouraged if a relative is hesitant to write down the family history. Any reply, no matter how simple, can be filed in your family genealogical archives and gives evidence of the place and time of residence of that particular family member. Patience is absolutely required in such matters and particularly when waiting to hear from a relative queried about individual histories. For some unknown reason, relatives who know the birth dates and marriage information of their children and grandchildren often take weeks and even years to write down what they know and reply to your inquiry. Sometimes a second carefully written letter of request is necessary to gather the information you are searching.

Failure to respond to your letter asking for genealogy information may sometimes be due to reluctance to divulge the truth in matters such as date of marriage. The older generations have not wanted to give out information if the first child was born too soon after wedlock. Recent generations are less concerned with what others think, and they easily accept what has happened.

Lack of knowledge of German cultural practices in the Old Country perhaps contributes to failure to respond. Divorce is another reason some people are reluctant to respond about personal history. Illegitimate or adopted children who bear the surname of the family should be reported as such and the fact can be noted in a footnote in family genealogy.

There may be a tendency to secretly hoard old family heirlooms to prevent jealousy of siblings or other relatives that will be encountered in your search to find clues to family history. Possessiveness can be an obsession when an heirloom is involved, whether or not the article has a monetary value. The greatest boon to finding heirlooms has been the recent surge to trace family roots. The popularity of genealogy has brought an increase in the visibility of treasured family heirlooms that suddenly appear with relatives or are talked about with pride. If that is not your experience, persistence and patience are necessary to search for ownership of a family Bible or other ancestral artifacts known to be in existence from clues given by a family member.

In German families it was traditional when a death occurred that an auction was held to sell possessions of the deceased person and divide the money gained among the legal benefactors. This tradition existed upon the death of a woman which meant household equipment, furniture, dishes, and personal possessions were sold to the highest bidder. It was impossible for a family member to own their mother's dishes, quilts, dining room cupboard, or silverware unless they had the money to outbid other competitors at the sale. The Bible in a family may have disappeared out of sight at one of these auctions and for many years its whereabouts or even its existence could go unknown. It was not uncommon for the family Bible containing records of dates and place of birth, marriages and deaths in Germany to never again be shown to relatives. In spite of such happening, it is possible for the genealogy researcher to find out all the information. It just takes more time, more persistence, and more patience.

Past generations of German families have been so mercenary as to sell "old things" because money was preferred to sentiment in the quest to attain the American Dream. Additionally, information may be held back if discrepancies in information become apparent. The discrepancies may only be simple errors and further research can easily resolve the problem. This is where you discover that searching for real facts is the adventure and challenge of the genealogist.

6. Sort information you have gathered into categories (a) yourself; (b) your father's family (paternal line); (c) your mother's family (maternal line). Create a chart:

PATERNAL – MATERNAL FAMILY LINES

	GRANDFATHER				GRAND-MOTHER		
SON	DAUGHTER	DAUGHTER	SON	SON	DAUGHTER	DAUGHTER	SON
CHILDEN	CHILDEN	CHILDEN	CHILDEN	CHILDEN	CHILDEN	CHILDEN	CHILDEN

Confusion often exists regarding relationships when you are trying to figure out how you are related to the people you are recording, or while you are discussing names with family members. Questions often arise, "How are you related to that person?" Do you know the difference between a first cousin and a first cousin-once-removed? The common expression "second cousin" is in many cases in reality a first cousin-once-removed to a genealogist. Your father's and mother's first cousins are your first cousins-once-removed which describes the number of generations you are away from your common ancestor. To understand relationships it is important to identify the common progenitor -- that grandparent who is the closest ancestor that two people have in common. For example, you and your first cousin do not have the same parents, but you have the same grandparent, your common progenitor.

A cousin is a child of your aunt and uncle, great-aunt, and great-uncle. If you know who your father's first cousin is, then you are that person's first cousin-once-removed. You are one generation away from that person. If you know who your grandfather's first cousin is, then you are two generations from that person, therefore, you are first cousins-twice-removed. In other words you have the same grandparents as your parents only you are more generations removed from them. In our country of only a little over two hundred years of history the "second" and "third" cousin designation common usage was an easy way of showing how many generations a person was away from their immigrant ancestor, and not a correct description of a genealogical relationship.

In both of my German grandparents' families there are a number of Krug cousins who married each other and a number of Happel cousins who married each other so that their grandchildren are their own fourth cousins.

To assist in understanding relationships, use this Relationship Chart:

1. Place the name of your common ancestor in the top block of the diamond.

2. Locate the position of yourself, or the family member, in the blocks on the top left side of the diamond.

3. Locate the position of the person whose relationship you are searching by finding his/her position in the blocks on the top right side of the diamond.

4. Your relationship will be where the two rows intersect.

RELATIONSHIP CHART

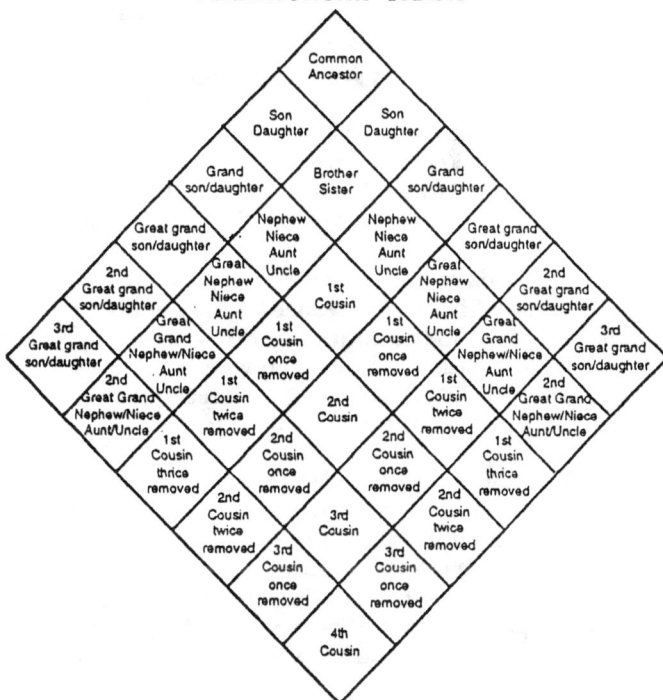

(Diamond-shaped relationship chart)

- Common Ancestor
- Son/Daughter — Son/Daughter
- Grand son/daughter — Brother/Sister — Grand son/daughter
- Great grand son/daughter — Nephew/Niece Aunt Uncle — Nephew/Niece Aunt Uncle — Great grand son/daughter
- 2nd Great grand son/daughter — Great Nephew Niece Aunt Uncle — 1st Cousin — Great Nephew Niece Aunt Uncle — 2nd Great grand son/daughter
- 3rd Great grand son/daughter — Great Grand Nephew/Niece Aunt Uncle — 1st Cousin once removed — 1st Cousin once removed — Great Grand Nephew/Niece Aunt Uncle — 3rd Great grand son/daughter
- 2nd Great Grand Nephew/Niece Aunt/Uncle — 1st Cousin twice removed — 2nd Cousin — 1st Cousin twice removed — 2nd Great Grand Nephew/Niece Aunt/Uncle
- 1st Cousin thrice removed — 2nd Cousin once removed — 2nd Cousin once removed — 1st Cousin thrice removed
- 2nd Cousin twice removed — 3rd Cousin — 2nd Cousin twice removed
- 3rd Cousin once removed — 3rd Cousin once removed
- 4th Cousin

After you have surveyed what you have gathered and sorted, and have contacted relatives who are willing to share information, you will have the basic information for a framework on which to build your German genealogy. You are now ready to begin the next step... actual research: looking for information you do not have.

7. Create a PEDIGREE CHART. (See page 49.) It will show any direct ancestor information that is missing. Search out your direct ancestors first. They are the foundation of any family record; then pursue collateral families if you so desire. If you have been able to find out the names of siblings of your grandparents, and the names of their children while visiting the elders in your family, you will be ready to draw more descendants' pedigree charts. It was fairly common in pioneer days for families to raise the orphaned children of another family. Sometimes children were adopted, and it is important to note that in your recordings. The hardships of pioneer life and the lack of health care shortened the lives of many women in early America. Family histories often include cases of men who married more than once and whose children were therefore half-siblings, having had the same father, but different mothers.

8. Visit the graves of ancestors and relatives for more clues. Cemeteries represent the history of people. German families have a tendency to remember only the paternal line because the Germanic culture is patrilineal. Not as much information is usually available about the early German women. You may need to search to find data about your grandmother's and great-grandmother's family lineage. The graves of German pioneer women in the 1800's were often unmarked by tombstones, making it necessary to search at ground level for a cement marker (See ground-level marker of immigrant Mother Krug, page 51). It may be necessary to find a cemetery plot book that records burials, to locate the graves of German women of earlier generations.

There are two kinds of cemetery records: gravestone inscriptions and cemetery records that specify exact location of burials. The lack of legal documents of German immigrant women in the United States -- due to automatic naturalization when their husbands were naturalized -- adds to the problem of finding recordings of full proper names, as well as birth and death dates for German immigrant women.

When families migrated from east to west in the United States, family history was scattered across many states. An ancestor born in Pennsylvania may be buried in Illinois where he/she made their home in later years with a son/daughter.

The bond between German family members and the church of their family heritage in the past was so strong that often a grandparent or relative resident from the Midwest retiring in California was

PEDIGREE CHART

(Father of No. 8)
(Mother of No. 8)
(Father of No. 9)
(Mother of No. 9)
(Father of No. 10)
(Mother of No. 10)
(Father of No. 11)
(Mother of No. 11)
(Father of No. 12)
(Mother of No. 12)
(Father of No. 13)
(Mother of No. 13)
(Father of No. 14)
(Mother of No. 14)
(Father of No. 15)
(Mother of No. 15)

(Father of No. 4)
(Mother of No. 4)
(Father of No. 5)
(Mother of No. 5)
(Father of No. 6)
(Mother of No. 6)
(Father of No. 7)
(Mother of No. 7)

(Father of No. 2)
(Mother of No. 2)
(Father of No. 3)
(Mother of No. 3)

(Father of No. 1)
(Mother of No. 1)

Date of birth
Place of birth
Date of marriage
Date of death
Place of death

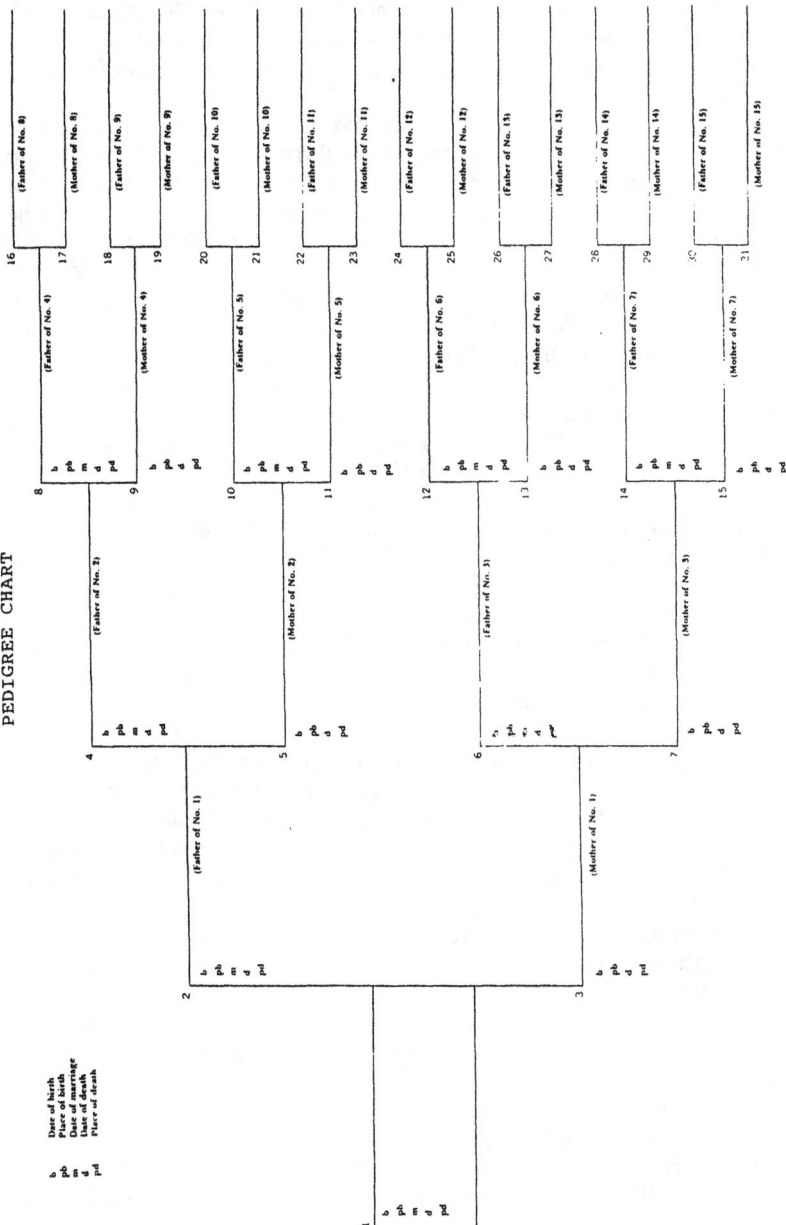

[49]

returned for burial with his/her ancestors in the family church cemetery in the Midwest. If you record details while talking with family members you will have clues to where to find the graves of your ancestors as you begin to understand the traditions of pioneer German families.

If your father, grandfather, or any older relative will go with you to the cemetery it is possible that you will discover new information about your family from recognition of tombstones of relatives not previously known or recorded. A considerable amount of time can be saved in searching for gravesites when an older member of the family accompanies you to the cemetery. When a grave of a direct descendant cannot be located, the older family member accompanying you can often guess what other cemetery might be the burial site for which you are searching. It's a good idea to take crayons and newsprint along to the cemetery to make tombstone rubbings to file with your genealogy records. It will save returning to the cemetery to look again at names, birth and death inscriptions, and epitaphs. Take a camera along and photograph the general location of the grave markers to make it easier to find family burial sites in future years. See the illustration on page 52, showing the English language name inscriptions on Krug immigrant gravesites, reflecting the strong desire to Americanize (Cathrine Krug-Anna Katharina Michel Krug and John Krug-Johann Peter Krug).

Viewing the cemetery with another member of the family provides the opportunity for more in-depth discussions of relationships of family members. Noting the location of graves also gives clues to family history and events. See the tombstone of immigrant Andreas Happel with German language inscriptions, *Gest. 8 Dec. 1895 Alter 74 Jahr, 8 Mo, 6 Tage*, page 53, and his immigrant son, *Johann Peter Happel Geb. 4 Maerz 1861, Gest. 13 Mai 1902*, page 54. When Johann Peter Happel's wife died 35 years later her children inscribed the tombstone simply in the English language for their immigrant mother Elizabeth (Katharina Elisabeth Werning) 1855-1937. Note the errors on the tombstone -- reversal of Peter's name from his baptized Peter Johann to Johann Peter, and Katharina Elisabeth's birth year in Germany is 1854 instead of 1855. The lack of documents in America to accurately pass information to relatives often resulted in errors in genealogical information recorded on cemetery markers and tombstones. Errors in oral tradition creep into family history at times of death.

9. Many German families in America have double cousins because more than one child in a family married children of another German family; for example, two Happel sisters of one family married two Krug brothers of the same family. In the Happel family five children in the immigrant family married five immigrant children of

Margaret Krug Palen searching for the cement ground-level marker of her immigrant great-great-grandmother, Anna Elisabeth (Paar) Krug, who died in 1882, seventeen years after coming to America.

Author Margaret Krug Palen stands beside
her immigrant Great Grandfather Johann Peter Krug's
English language tombstone.

Margaret Krug Palen standing beside the tombstone of her immigrant great-great-grandfather, Andreas Happel. German language inscription: *Gest 3 Dec 1895 Alter 74 Jahre 8 Mo 6 Tage*, and a Bible verse in German.

IMMIGRANTS' GERMAN LANGUAGE TOMBSTONE:
Peter Johann Happel's tombstone reversed his baptized name to: JOHANN
PETER HAPPEL *Geb. 4 Maerz 1851, Gest. 13 Mai 1902.* His wife's baptized
name, Katharina Elisabeth (Werning) Happel was changed to: ELIZABETH
HAPPEL 1855-1937. Records in Germany show she was born in 1854. Such
errors often occur due to lack of primary documents of immigrants in this
country.

IMMIGRANTS' ENGLISH LANGUAGE HEADSTONES
Headstone markers indicate the names commonly used in America
to relate to future generations.

the Rinderknecht family making it possible for cousins to be their own cousin. To understand relationships, study this Consanguinity Chart using the information you have gathered. Fill in the space that reads YOUR NAME. Write in the names of your parents, grandparents, great-grandparents, etc., and descendants.

Table of Consanguinity

Numbers show degree of relationship

					GREAT GREAT GREAT GRANDPARENTS (5)
				GREAT GREAT GRANDPARENTS (4)	GREAT GREAT GRAND UNCLES AUNTS (6)
			GREAT GRANDPARENTS (3)	GREAT GRAND UNCLES AUNTS (5)	FIRST COUSINS THRICE REMOVED (7)
		GRANDPARENTS (2)	GREAT UNCLES AUNTS (4)	FIRST COUSINS TWICE REMOVED (6)	SECOND COUSINS TWICE REMOVED (8)
	PARENTS (1)	UNCLES AUNTS (3)	FIRST COUSINS ONCE REMOVED (5)	SECOND COUSINS ONCE REMOVED (7)	THIRD COUSINS ONCE REMOVED (9)
YOUR NAME	BROTHERS SISTERS (2)	FIRST COUSINS (4)	SECOND COUSINS (6)	THIRD COUSINS (8)	FOURTH COUSINS (10)
CHILDREN (1)	NEPHEWS NIECES (3)	FIRST COUSINS ONCE REMOVED (5)	SECOND COUSINS ONCE REMOVED (7)	THIRD COUSINS ONCE REMOVED (9)	FOURTH COUSINS ONCE REMOVED (11)
GRAND CHILDREN (2)	GRAND NEPHEWS NIECES (4)	FIRST COUSINS TWICE REMOVED (6)	SECOND COUSINS TWICE REMOVED (8)	THIRD COUSINS TWICE REMOVED (10)	FOURTH COUSINS TWICE REMOVED (12)
GREAT-GRAND CHILDREN (3)	GREAT-GRAND NEPHEWS NIECES (5)	FIRST COUSINS THRICE REMOVED (7)	SECOND COUSINS THRICE REMOVED (9)	THIRD COUSINS THRICE REMOVED (11)	FOURTH COUSINS THRICE REMOVED (13)

In Germany it was common in past generations for villagers to marry cousins when transportation did not exist to travel to meet people from other areas. A European tradition prohibits young men from courting young women of villages other than their own or they become subjected to harassment by the men of their own village. An exception, young people from small villages without churches where villagers walked to the next village to be members of a mother church, resulted in young people of neighboring villages of those congregations marrying.

Do not be surprised in searching village records in Germany back into the 1600's, together with German family marriages in your American family, to find you are your own cousin. For example, if your great-grandparents were first cousins when they married, you are your own fourth cousin. A number of families in the Krug and Happel descendants can trace their ancestry in this manner.

10. Fit all the clues you have gathered together. Have you located the name of your immigrant German ancestor and place of residence in Germany? Every German family in the United States has immigrant ancestors. It's important to identify the members of your family who emigrated from Germany: names, date of arrival in the United States, where they lived and worked. It is fascinating to find out where your forebears lived, the kind of work they did, the town, or farm where they lived. Your search should exhaust all available sources in the United States to find the place of origin of your ancestors in Germany. You may even wish to visit the homes of your ancestors of earlier years.

The oldest living member of a family is the best source of clues if you need to recheck family data. Memories, anecdotes and sayings remembered from grandparents, possibly great-grand ancestors give valuable leads to identification of your immigrant ancestor. Sometimes there are differences in memory among family members. Distortion of facts or fantasy may have crept into oral history through the generations.

It is not uncommon for an amateur genealogist to claim to be able to trace family roots back to the 1600's or even to an earlier century. However, do not believe everything you hear or read. The large amount of effort required to trace family roots and an impatient need for satisfaction and progress causes many genealogy buffs to rush to get back as far as possible or to latch onto a branch of some prestigious family tree.

Although searching primary sources takes extra time and money, it is worth the investment. Following the most direct genealogy path uncovers the most accurate facts. Secondary records such as lists of wills, lists of land claims or even published family genealogies, often contain mistakes. The time and money taken to search primary records may reveal a second marriage as well as other inconsistencies. Caution should be taken to realize that primary records are not totally accurate either, for example, birth certificates with inaccuracies when the baby's names were not decided upon at time of birth or were unknown by the person filling out the certificate.

When family histories are repeated from generation to generation, without written records, members tend to embellish the facts. They may clean up some details and drop others. A person said to have been a gold miner may turn out to have been a horse trader.

SUMMARY: Genealogy progress takes time and is not super simple. You are the detective and it is necessary to listen carefully for "leads" to more discoveries. If a family clue says that your ancestor was in the Civil War, research to find out if it is true. Oral tradition in genealogy findings must be verified using primary and secondary sources. Primary sources are vital in reconstructing family lineage and are made by the ancestor or persons involved in the event or in proximity to the occasion. Check at least two sources, preferably three, whenever possible to compare for accuracy. Secondary sources are records made by people who were not eyewitnesses or at a later time did not have access to a primary source. All secondary sources must be verified to find out if they are correct.

The challenge of the genealogist is to distinguish between fiction and facts in primary and secondary sources. This requires patience and sometimes a little imagination. However, there are many rewards including a new-found closeness to family and friends met along the way.

Evaluate your research as you go along to find answers to the following questions:

Is there a written genealogy in your family?

Does anyone have old family documents or artifacts?

Who were the immigrants in your German family?

Where did your immigrant ancestors live in America?

What was your German ancestor's occupation in America?

How did immigrant ancestors deal with life in the New World?

Names of organizations connected with immigrant ancestors?

Are there old photographs?

RESEARCH CHECK LIST

Name:

Relationship:

Parents:

Location of sources:

Type of source:

Date of source:

Miscellaneous Records

☐ Home

☐ Family Bible

☐ Family letters

☐ Photographs

☐ Interviews

County records

☐ Birth record

☐ Marriage records

☐ Wills, estates

☐ Deeds, Mortgages

☐ Naturalization records

Town records

☐ Cemetery recs, inscripts.

☐ Newspaper files

☐ Tax lists

☐ Voter records

☐ Public school records

Church records

☐ Local church histories

☐ Local parish records

☐ Cemetery, grave inscript.

State records

☐ Vital records

☐ Land grants

☐ State census

☐ Militia records

☐ Tax lists

☐ Archives

National records

☐ Censuses

☐ Military records

☐ Pension records

☐ Passenger lists

☐ Immigration records

☐ Land records

Libraries

☐ Indexes

☐ City or county directories

☐ Printed genealogies

☐ Histories

☐ Biographical compendia

☐ Manuscript histories

☐ Obit collections, indexes

☐ Cemetery recs, inscripts.

☐ Abstract volumes

[4]

When Your Ancestor's Origin in Germany is Unknown

Every German family in America has immigrant ancestors, but for many years it was common to forget who they were, because immigrants were looked down upon and considered unimportant when compared to the descendants of colonists and early pioneer families.

The area of origin or locality of German immigrants is often one of the most difficult things to discover. To trace German ancestors, the methods of researching forgotten ancestors needs to be studied. The best time to do this is before attempting any research in Europe.

Many German families saved memorabilia that may help sort out the necessary information. To carry out research, start from what you know and use that information to find more clues to your family's roots. Then you will discover that every family's circumstances are different. In every stage of research, the next step will be determined by what you have found out. Your detective work will lead you from one step to the next. There are no shortcuts, for example, finding a family genealogy of earlier years of the same surname and trying to extend it forward to connect it with your family. The only way you can make a connection, if there is a connection with that family, is by adding to your own family information and working backwards. Search in old scrapbooks that contain obituaries, accounts of weddings, reunion news stories, and photos that may give clues to research that will uncover answers to these questions:

- Who was your immigrant ancestor(s)?
- Where did your German ancestors live in the Old World?
- What was the occupation of your family in Germany?
- What was it like in Germany when your ancestors lived there?
- What was your family's religion in Germany?
- What conditions encouraged your ancestors to leave Germany?
- Are there descriptions of emigration in your family?
- What was the European port of emigration?
- What was the name of the ship that brought them to America?
- Do you know when your family arrived in America?
- How old were your ancestor(s) upon arrival in America?
- Where did your ancestor(s) go when they got off the ship?
- Was there contact with relatives and friends in Germany?

Waves of German emigrants in the nineteenth century carried few possessions with them when they left Germany for the New World. They took no documents or maps of Germany when they left their homeland.

Germans came to North America to find new opportunities to improve their economic condition, to avoid compulsory military conscription, and to avoid depressions, famine, revolution and religious conflicts. The two wars with Germany in the twentieth century silenced German naturalized citizens, causing them to cease talking about the place where they lived in the Old Country. Many German families preferred to forget their origin and ancestry in the Old Country and concentrate on counting their blessings of living in America. This cultural alienation caused many Germanic people to feel that their descendants didn't care to know about the life and times of their ancestors. Patriotism in their American homeland superseded memories of Germany. Many German immigrants in North America carried the knowledge of their place of origin in Germany, the location of their birth and residence in their homeland to the grave with them. This can be frustrating for the genealogy researcher when family members either are not cooperative in giving out information or claim to have forgotten everything they heard years ago, or even hesitate to write down what they may possibly remember.

Without the name of a specific village or city in Germany, the search for your German roots is likely to end at the Atlantic Ocean. This can happen even when you know the name of your immigrant ancestors. In most cases, the place of origin of your ancestors can be found somewhere in American records. An obituary clipped out of the newspaper and saved in old letters or in the family Bible is often the place to find the location in Germany of the residence of your immigrant ancestors. Without that information it will be difficult, probably impossible, to research your family's origin in Germany.

Usually, the first generation born in North America remembers what the immigrant parents from Germany told them about their homeland, and that often is also your family's last place of residence before emigration. If that information was not written down, the second and third generation born in the United States probably have lost the memory of the exact village or city of origin in Germany of the immigrant ancestor. Great-Uncle George Krug often told what he remembered his immigrant father describing in Germany.

German ancestry researchers of the second generation or later, born in the United States, often only know that their immigrant ancestors came from Germany. Americanization is the quest of the lifetime for the second generation born in North America. In the process of Americanizing, many details of the Old Country are forgotten or shoved aside as no longer important. If the name of the immigrant ancestor or the exact village or place of residence to research is not known, to continue finding family history in Germany it is important to make a thorough search specifically to find clues. Begin with the names you have collected to make a starting point in a search for records. There are archives, libraries, and records depositories -- local, state, regional, and national -- that will provide clues to the immigrants in your family. Follow these steps:

♦ 1. Family clues - probe your relatives, close and distant. Write, telephone or visit relatives to try to jog memories of older family members to find out what they remember hearing said about their immigrant ancestor's name and arrival in the United States. Often German immigrants lived for a period of time with other German families already settled in a community until they could settle and acquire a place of their own in the New World. German families survived and prospered in the newly developing country when they resided in clusters in American communities. Hunt for clues among other German families in the same community for the name of the village or city in Germany that was the residence of your ancestors in the Old Country. Often many of the settlers of a community in the United States were immigrants from the same or nearby places in Germany.

It was traditional in the nineteenth century and early twentieth century to embroider quilts at bridal showers with names of relatives and close friends. Maiden names and other information may be recorded on quilt blocks that exist as cherished heirlooms in family trunks and attics. Examine quilts and needlework samplers for names, ages and other historical data worked into the designs.

♦ 2. Church records in the United States - pastors, priests and ministers of community churches recorded baptisms or christenings, confirmations, communions (See page 65), weddings, deaths and burials in a church register in the German language until the twentieth century. Unless someone can read handwritten German script, it is often difficult to decipher the records. Finding the name and date of an ancestor registered for communion may be an important clue to exact name and/or time of residence in the community/country. Church bulletins, old newsletters printed over the years, and centennial booklets contain old photos and historical sketches that may give further clues about your family.

♦ 3. Naturalization records - the process by which an alien becomes a citizen was conducted before September 26, 1906 in any court -

federal, state or local. The records are found in the court where the naturalization took place (See pages 67, 68). Naturalization was not always required for a person to live in the United States, therefore, some immigrants were never naturalized.

From 1790 to 1795 the residence requirement for naturalization was one year in a state and two years in the United States. In 1795 a change required residency of five years in the United States. From 1798 to 1802 a fourteen-year residency in the United States was required and a Declaration of Intention had to be filed five years prior to naturalization. In 1802 laws changed requirements back to one year's residence in a state and five years in the United States with a Declaration of Intention filed three years prior to naturalization. Some immigrants declared their legal intention to become citizens, but never went through the final paperwork. Great-Great-Grandfather Adam Werning, age 64 years, swore an Oath of Intention 24 August 1876. He died in 1879 before taking out final naturalization papers. (See page 66.)

The data required for an Oath of Intention to become a naturalized citizen in the nineteenth century varied from jurisdiction to jurisdiction. The County Courthouse Record Clerk's Office naturalization records verify if immigrant ancestors lived in Germany or the part of Germany known as Prussia. Methods of recording naturalization varied from county to county. See the examples on pages 67 and 68: John Krug, naturalization 4 March 1873, indicating Oath of Intention 28 February 1871 (Benton County, IA); and Andrew Happel, naturalization 28 October 1875, indicating Oath of Naturalization 25 March 1872 (Linn Co., IA).

In 1906 naturalization was standardized by the federal government, and records after that time are available from the Immigration and Naturalization Service, Washington D.C. Naturalization records provide names of the new citizen's spouse and children, date and place of arrival in the U.S.

In the nineteenth century and until 1922, married females were automatically naturalized when their husbands were naturalized, therefore, it is impossible to find naturalization records of immigrant women. Unmarried females could go through the naturalization process, but few apparently did for a variety of unknown reasons. In 1973 the U.S. Congress passed a law making naturalization records accessible to the public. Since that time more records have been published and can be located on genealogy shelves in libraries throughout the country, making it easier to search German roots.

♦ 4. Newspapers - every American community that published a newspaper gave accounts of family happenings, thereby recording important genealogical information such as dates and places of births, marriages, and burials; obituaries; announcements of family reunions, birthday celebrations, and community events. City and county libraries have newspaper collections that sometimes go back to the first issues published. Marriage announcements and obituaries in these old issues often contain crucial family history clues such as the German birthplace or residence of your ancestors. Newspaper stories list cemetery names, mortuaries, and hospitals -- all of which are sources to check for further clues.

♦ 5. Death certificates - fees are charged for certificates, and the information on them varies from state to state: date and hour of death, cause and place of death, home address and age of the deceased, place of residence, marital status and name of spouse, birth date and birthplace if known, name of father and maiden name of mother if known, birthplace of father and mother if known, name of funeral home (another place to check records for missing information). If information was furnished by a relative, that name will also appear on the death certificate.

♦ 6. Other immigration records - researchers often spend a large amount of time and energy scanning ship passenger lists to determine the ship their immigrant ancestor(s) crossed the Atlantic Ocean on only to discover that the lists seldom give the name of the village or city of emigration. In most instances emigrants traveled a distance from their native village or city to a port city to sail to America. However, the ship passenger lists verify the port of embarkation and name of the ship plus the date of debarkation. Many Germans sailed from Bremen or Hamburg, the two main ports of embarkation in Germany, but they were seldom their hometown.

If your ancestor(s) sailed between 1850 and 1934 from Hamburg, Germany, the ship passenger lists often include the specific village or city of residence and often contain the country, province or region in Germany from which the passenger emigrated. Ship passenger lists are indexed and are available at many public libraries and genealogical society libraries, or on microfilm at the Family History Library in Salt Lake City, or through satellite LDS Family History Centers located throughout the country. The National Archives in Washington D.C. has passenger lists available for public search. These lists were filed by masters of ships with port officials according to the requirements of the March 2, 1819 Act of Congress. New York, Philadelphia and Baltimore were ports of entry for many German immigrants.

If your ancestor's exact date of arrival and name of the ship are unknown, don't give up. If you even know the approximate date of arrival, the port of embarkation, or the port of arrival -- or any combination of these -- you can consult directories available at the National Archives and all major libraries that list ship-by-ship dates of arrival in New York 1890-1930, and Baltimore, Boston, and Philadelphia in 1904-1926. Check local and state library volumes of passenger lists before searching elsewhere.

♦ 7. Land records - may provide the clue you are seeking to verify the name of your immigrant ancestor and his or her residence after arrival in the United States. Search for warrant appeals, jury records, surveyor and boundary records, tax records, probate and court records, maps, state institution records, military records, pension records, health and welfare records, business and license records, school and school board records.

♦ 8. National Archives - search yourself or hire someone to do it for you. Local genealogical societies and libraries, and state libraries can provide the correct mailing address in Washington D.C. to request a detailed list of types of records available to the family historian, including military and census records. Computer-literate genealogists may check the Internet to see what lists are available. The archives on Revolutionary soldiers attempting to collect pensions may list the source of income as well as assets, age, and names and ages of wife and children. The Federal Government has taken a census of the entire population in the United States every ten years beginning with 1790, listing each household and person including babies, children, relatives, slaves, elderly dependents identified by age, gender, and place of birth, along with value of real estate and personal estate, whether they could read or write, physical disabilities etc. A "Soundex" census (an index of phonetically sounded-out surnames) is available for each state, to assist in locating immigrant ancestor(s) or in searching for other people with your last name.

♦ 9. Probate records - the last will and testament of a relative is a valuable genealogical source to determine the name of your immigrant ancestor(s), because the names of relatives are listed. All wills are available to the public once they are filed after death of the writer. Probate laws are different in some states, but most wills are filed in the local county courthouse. Today, as in earlier days, if death occurs without a will and the deceased owned property, the court appoints an administrator to dispose of the property, and that record is also on file and open to the public.

Atkins, Iowa, Parish Communion Register

NATURALIZATION OF ALIENS.

United States of America

STATE OF IOWA, Benton County.

BEFORE THE CLERK of the _____ Court appeared, _____ a native of _____ aged _____ years, who being duly sworn, upon his oath declares that it is bona fide his intention to become a citizen of the United States, and to renounce forever all allegiance and fidelity to every Prince, Potentate, State and Sovereignty whatsoever, and particularly to _____ of whom he is at present a subject.

Sworn to and subscribed before me this _____ day of _____ 1876.

_____ Clerk.
By _____ Deputy.

BEFORE THE CLERK of the _____ Court appeared _____ a native of _____ aged _____ years, who being duly sworn, upon his oath declares that it is bona fide his intention to become a citizen of the United States, and to renounce forever all allegiance and fidelity to every Prince, Potentate, State and Sovereignty whatsoever, and particularly to _____ of whom he is at present a subject.

Sworn to and subscribed before me this _____ day of _____ 187_.

_____ Clerk.
By _____ Deputy.

BEFORE THE CLERK of the _____ Court appeared _____ a native of _____ aged _____ years, who being duly sworn, upon his oath declares that it is bona fide his intention to become a citizen of the United States, and to renounce forever all allegiance and fidelity to every Prince, Potentate, State and Sovereignty whatsoever, and particularly to _____ of whom he is at present a subject.

Sworn to and subscribed before me this _____ day of _____ 187_.

_____ Clerk.
By _____ Deputy.

Oath of Naturalization Intention

Naturalization Record, Benton County, Iowa

NATURALIZATION

Names.	Nature of Application.	Month.	Day.	Year.
Happel Andrew *Prussia*	First oath of naturalization filed before clerk & c.	March	25	1872
	Admitted as a citizen of the U.S.	October	28	1875
Hill William L *from England*	First oath of naturalization filed.	Apr	10	1872
	Final Papers. 3-124	Jany	5	1878
Hinkley Edwin	First oath of naturalization filed	October	15	1872
Horak John	First oath taken befor			1867
	Final oath + admission to Citizenship before Circuit Court Linn Co Iowa	Jany	7	1873
Hansen Jesse	Admitted to citizenship	January	5	1875
Hansen Frederick	Admitted as a citizen of the U.S.	January	5	1875
Hovis John	Admitted to citizenship	January	21	1875

Original: Linn Co. Courthouse Cedar Rapids, Iowa

Naturalization Record of Andrew Happel, Linn County, Iowa

♦ 10. Cemeteries - if research leads to a grave of a person you are not sure is an ancestor, make notes on date of death, age, and any other inscribed information such as "father." A search of the cemetery records will show where the person died. With that information it is possible to obtain the person's death certificate, which tells the names of the parents of the deceased. That is sufficient information to search for a will. Another place to look is is in the obituary section of back issues of the local newspaper. In the newly developing Midwest and West, several years passed before the tax levies could support and justify the expansion of county record keeping beyond naturalization and court proceedings. Deaths were not recorded until later in the twentieth century. Immigrants who were not members of a church were buried privately on their own land and left no trace of their demise other than possibly a tombstone. Some early immigrants can only be traced through records of organized early pioneer cemeteries. Remember that there was a strong desire among German immigrant families to marry within their own religion and to shun the unchurched, therefore, church cemetery records are the place to search.

♦ 11. Surname searches - if all else fails, search your family surname. If the surname is a common one, it may be most helpful to search the husband's surname first, followed by a search of the wife's maiden surname. Surname books list many German families and the villages and cities of their origin. Consult the nearest local branch of LDS Family Records Center for assistance. There are many satellites of the Family History Library which the Church of Jesus Christ of Latter-day Saints (Mormon) maintains in Salt Lake City, Utah. Each center has computer access to everything in Salt Lake City. The Mormon religion places great importance on genealogical documentation, and the family history centers are open to the public and free of charge. Their archives in Salt Lake City, Utah have volumes of indexed surnames. Search the spelling of your surname. Different records may have different spellings. Birth records and church records may be spelled differently. The difference in spelling may be phonetic. Years ago many people had limited education and county clerks may have made a record based upon the pronunciation of the name, using phonetic spelling. If a German name was Americanized, it may be found spelled more than one way in old records.

♦ 12. County histories - information about immigrant ancestors listed in county histories usually contains the place of the immigrant's origin in Germany. In addition, religion, political affiliation, occupation, business, and names of family members may be given in biographical sketches.

♦ 13. Genealogical Societies - local genealogical societies are a resource for tracking families because they have records from other people who have conducted searches. Often a person finds that their family tree ties into one that has already been already researched. Most genealogical societies have excellent library collections and materials to assist in research work.

♦ 14. City Directories - serve the purpose of identifying people by name and address. City directories have been published by many cities and towns since the 1800s. Check the local public library or state library collection to search for your immigrant family and their occupation, old addresses, wife's name, clues to arrival in an area etc.

SUMMARY - There are many clues that yield valuable information to finding your immigrant ancestors and their residence in Germany. Upon arrival in America, German families pursued religious values that prepared them for the hard work ethic and death. They sought land in the same general area and organized around a nucleus to form religious congregations and build churches. Records kept in early organized churches are a primary source for locating immigrant names and native villages in Germany. Your research should yield the following information:

Original surname
Religion
Place and date of birth, marriage, death, burial
Place of last residence in Germany
Port of departure in Europe
Occupation
Date and Port of Entry in North America, name of ship
Place of residence after arrival
Naturalization date
Education
Military service
Economic circumstances
Language(s) spoken

Add to your family tree data to trace your immigrant ancestors in this order:
1. Information held by yourself and relatives.
2. Records created by local, state and U.S. governments.
3. Church and other records.

[5]

Locating Your Ancestral Roots in Germany

The task of tracing German ancestors can appear daunting. By the time you get back to your great-great-grandparents, there are thirty-one individuals over four generations on your family tree. It is really impossible to trace ancestry in Germany until you know the specific village your ancestors came from in the Old Country. Most German ancestors of Americans came from villages, not large cities or capitals, however, a large city in Germany is frequently mentioned in family oral tradition as a recognizable place for identification purposes. The agricultural population of Germany lives in villages (See View of Löhlbach, page 74) and works on the land surrounding the area, in contrast to individual farm homes on the farmland in North America.

It is important to examine your research findings to see if you located the place of birth or last village of residence in Germany of your immigrant ancestor. In most instances there are family records that give the name of the ancestral village recorded in a newspaper obituary, on a tombstone, in old letters or in the family Bible. If tracing your German roots has led to discovery of the specific village of residence of your ancestors, a thorough search must be made in Germany to determine the accuracy of the location of the village and where records repositories may be found.

Many places in Germany have the same name. A county, township or forest in Europe is called a duchy or principality. More than one village in Germany has the same name though located in different provinces, now called states. Adding to the problem is the fact that German records are rarely centralized and seldom indexed. The ravages of war in parts of Germany have caused some records to be gathered in other parts of the country.

After collecting all the information and oral tradition you can find about your family in the United States, and locating the immigrant ancestor, you are ready to search your roots in Germany. To trace ancestors in the Old Country, knowledge of names, villages of residence, and the time period when they lived in Germany is not enough to predict what can be found out about your family in Europe. Knowledge of the geographical location in Germany and historical influences on that area impact the availability of information that can be discovered in a genealogical search. Locating

German ancestral roots is exciting. It is fascinating to find out where your forebears lived, the kind of work they did, what their homes were like (See Bauernstube, page 75), and what the village of residence is like (See Battenhausen, page 108). It may even be possible to determine whether the old house your ancestors lived in is still standing. (See fachverk Happel home, pages 76-77.)

The greatest satisfaction in locating your ancestral roots in Germany results from contacts with distant relatives and German friends not previously met. See page 78 for a photograph of visit in Dankerode-on-der-Fulda home of Great-Great-Great Grandfather Johann Valentine Werning with engraved foundation stone of his name and date 1833. A relative of his daughter-in-law, Great-Grandmother Katharina Elisabeth Happel nee Werning, lives in the home and cares for the pewter baptismal bowl and communion ware used in the Dankerode Church (built 1691) just across the street from the home. It was exciting to see the baptismal bowl and communion set, used in the church since 1733, the same one used by Werning ancestors before emigrating to America.

Villagers in Germany speak only the German language, though village school children now study English. Don't.be discouraged if you cannot speak, read or write German. When I was growing up in a Midwestern ethnic German farming community, father admonished, "If anyone says 'Gesundheit' to you, respond, 'Dankeschön.'" The word "Gesundheit" was considered an essential part of a good education in our old-fashioned and God-fearing family. It was the only German word we were permitted to know and use, attesting to our good manners. Today in Germany, the response is simply the informal, "Danke." Dankeschön is a formal expression. The German community of my birth and youth determined, following World War I, that the younger generation would have English as a first language, and made sure conversations with youth never included any German words, with the exception of "Gesundheit."

In a bilingual family, when the first language is not the same in generations of the same family, it is really difficult for many to understand that there are different ways of thinking, also different patterns of communication going on in the family at the same time. Researching and studying family genealogy gives new insight and understandings to why this difference happens.

It is important to know whether the progenitor you are tracing was Protestant or Catholic. Protestants were either Lutheran, Evangelical or Reformed. Research in Germany is complicated because of the kingdoms which divided the country, and religious differences which fragmented the division. Bavaria and the Rhineland are Catholic; northern and eastern Germany are Lutheran.

A positive factor in searching Germanic roots is that Germany was the first European nation to develop the scientific aspects of genealogy. Genealogy records were not a privilege accorded only to the German nobility. Village churches in Germany contain collections of baptism, confirmation, marriage, death and burial records including notations on family relationships, emigration dates of individuals and families. A negative factor is the many wars that swept through Germany over centuries changing the borders of the country, also destroyed many villages and church records. In spite of the destruction caused by many wars, diligence in German genealogy research reveals valuable insight into conditions that caused ancestors to emigrate from their native land. German history is complex compared to the two hundred years of U.S. history, however, every Germanic family in America has had an encounter with war, both in Europe and/or North America. American-German families are familiar with what happened in The Revolutionary War, Civil War, World Wars I and II, Korean War, Vietnam War, but often little is known about the wars that ravaged Germany impacting Germanic family histories.

A significant factor in tracing my German Krug family emigration to America in 1865 was the Prussian War and the annexing of Hessen-Kassel to Prussia in 1866. My great-grandfather was twenty-one years old in 1865, the age at which military service in the Prussian War became compulsory. Other significant factors were friends and relatives of the Krug family, immigrants to Iowa in earlier years, sending correspondence to Germany notifying my Krug family that President Abraham Lincoln signed the 1864 Homestead Act to disperse lands in the Louisiana Purchase west of the Mississippi River. Then it was possible to purchase farmland in Iowa.

In the event that you have not found a specific village name with the discovery of the name of your immigrant ancestor, trace names of other German families in the same community of your family residence, or other related German surnames in your direct family lineage. Following arrival in North America, German families often settled in the same communities and married children of other families from Germany. This happened when early German arrivals corresponded with their friends and relatives still living in Germany and related the golden opportunities of owning land in America, thus enticing and increasing emigration from the Old Country.

It is important to realize that your family members undoubtedly have different names, either Christian first names or surnames, or both, in Germany than in the United States. German surnames may be clues to place of origin, residence, occupation or contain a prefix or a suffix of regional significance. The spelling of many surnames changed over the years of immigration due to phonetic sound when

VIEW OF LÖHLBACH IN THE KELLERWALD

1870 Bauernstube (Farmer's Home)

House in Altenhaina, built in 1813 by Johann Peter Happel, one year after his marriage to Anna Gertrud Fackiner of Altenhaina. The inscription painted on the front of the fachverk house reads "built in year 1813, 3 July by master carpenter from Löhlbach Johann Peter Happel."

Andreas Happel was born in this house, 27 March 1821,
and emigrated to America in 1864.

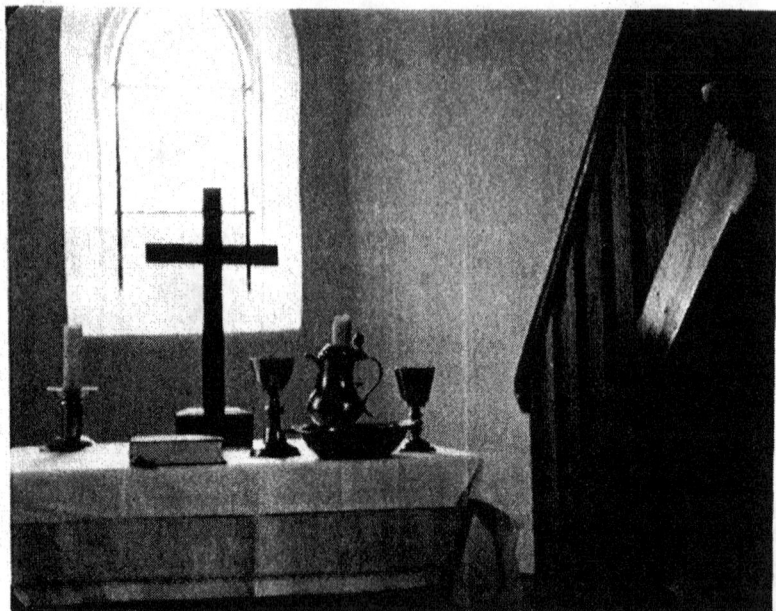

Pewter Communion set and baptismal bowl used continuously since 1633 and still in use at the church built in 1691 in Dankerode-on-der-Fulda.

Willie Knierin shows Margaret Krug Palen the pewter set used by her Werning ancestors. They are in the Werning home in Dankerode where Adam Werning and his family lived before emigrating to America.

spoken, length of the name, or difficulty in spelling or pronunciation by second parties writing documents. Pressure to Americanize, or mistakes in transcribing by officials were common causes of changes in names. During this period, many immigrants lacked education upon arrival and little concern was given to acquiring an education in a developing country where economic opportunities were available for the taking. Fortunately, many German surnames are uncommon and it is possible to easily make a connection with a particular region of Germany because the name is often found in that area of of the country.

Many German-Americans purposely made changes in their names using phonetic spelling at the time of naturalization to anglicize their surnames. Clues to surname changes must be found before starting research in Germany. If all the steps listed in the chapter on searching German roots have been thoroughly followed, any significant changes in family names will have been discovered.

Some of the more common changes made to German names in America are as follows: the *umlaut* (two dots) was usually dropped from a vowel and an "e" was added immediately following the vowel, thus ü became ue, ö became oe; and ä became ae; ie and ei were interchanged for convenient phonetic pronunciation; the German consonant combination pf was changed to either p, ph, or f in America; g in German was changed to k; k in German was changed to c or ch in the spelling of a surname in North America. Thus Andreas became Andrew; Johanna or Hanna became Jane; Johannes or Johann became John; Georg and Juergen became George; Franz became Frank; Anna became Ann etc. "Lizzy" and "Katie" were common American nicknames for the German names Elisabeth and Katharina.

Europeans did not have surnames until about 1000 A.D. Surnames developed as population growth made it necessary to identify people according to place, occupation, nickname, or patronyms (meaning son of). Early genealogy recordings in parts of Germany give only one Christian first name for men, Johann or Johannes, and either Elisabeth or Katharina for women. The genealogy buff should expect to find many ancestors in searches with the same name or the same names in a different order. For example, Johann Heinrich and Heinrich Johann or Katharina Elisabeth and Elisabeth Katharina. In earlier centuries families had many children and frequently more than one child had the same name. In the early seventeenth century to mid-nineteenth century, German village families tended to use necronyms -- the names of deceased siblings. Families continued using the same Christian names from one generation to the next. A lack of medical care in village life and lack of birth control resulted in large village families with deaths of many children at young ages. Seventeenth- and eighteenth-century records in Germany also contain deaths of many women during childbirth, resulting in the remarriage of men and many half-sibling recordings to be traced in family histories.

In Germany it was common to nickname family members to distinguish one person from the other when so many in the same family had the same names. A common German nickname for Johann the son of Johann was Henry. Thus the phrase, "Write your John Henry" became a popular and common saying in America when requesting the signature of a German person.

Germans in America favored naming sons after Teutonic warriors, Frankish nobility, and English Kings. Favorite names were: William, Richard, Edward, George, Karl, Charles, August, Henry, Conrad. Daughters were given names of Christian saints and names that were traditional in the English culture: Margaret, Jane, Catherine, Frances, Mary, Elizabeth and Anne.

If you have searched all family records, and obituary records in newspapers of the communities of your relatives (many public libraries have a list of newspapers, 1821-1936, compiled by Winfield Gregory), and still are unable to trace a village of birth or residence of your ancestors in Germany, make a thorough search of passenger lists or naturalization records, county histories where your ancestors lived, and census records.

Before starting research to trace ancestors in Germany:

♦ 1. Gather research materials - manila file folders labeled one for each branch of the family that will be searched. Keep correspondence and materials collected both before and after research in Germany in the individual family file folders that are lightweight and easy to carry. Take them with you when you travel abroad.

♦ 2. German Language Dictionary - valuable reference for both genealogy record searching by mail and travel abroad.

♦ 3. German Genealogy Guides and Dictionaries - publications of German family records on a dictionary basis are excellent references when researching in Germany. (See Bibliogrpahy: Byler, Palen, Tolzmann.)

♦ 4. Pedigree Chart - make a pedigree chart, see page 49, and fill in as much as possible before tracing your roots in Germany by mail or traveling to Europe to begin research. A pedigree chart helps keep the generations separated starting with yourself. This is especially useful when records show generations with the same or similar names. It also shows where to begin research and where there are genealogy problems to search out.

♦ 5. Family Sheets - necessary to record complete family groups, listing information about parents and children. Plan to have a generous supply in your research portfolios.

♦ 6. Know the difference between the Julian calendar and the Gregorian calendar before starting research in Europe. The calendar was invented in Egypt 6,000 years ago. When Julius Caesar adopted the Egyptian calendar in Rome, the existing Roman calendar had only ten months or 288 days. To adjust it to the Egyptian calendar they had to add two months. These new months were named Juli after Julius Caesar and August after Caesar Augustus. Instead of adding them to the end of the year they pushed them into the middle of the year because Julius Caesar was born in the middle of the year. The Egyptian December (Dece means ten) was the tenth month on the Egyptian calendar; October means eight and was moved to the tenth month; September means seven and was moved to the ninth month. The Romans did not care about the meaning of the names of the ten months. They readjusted the month of July to have 31 days for Julius Caesar. The 24-hour day we know is taken from the 24 gates in the Egyptian Book of the Dead.

The Julian calendar, established by Julius Ceasar, was used from 325 to 1582 A.D. After the discovery that a mistake had been made in calculating the length of the solar year it became necessary to change the calendar year to coincide with the sun. Pope Gregory XIII in 1582 ordered the calendar changed to the correct date of the equinox. Relations between England and the Pope were strained; therefore, the new Gregorian calendar was not officially adopted by English-speaking people (including the English colonies) until 1752, when the difference between the sun and the calendar had grown to eleven days. Whenever double dates appear in early genealogy records in Germany or North America, such as 9 February 1743/44, it refers to both the Julian and the Gregorian calendars. That can explain the difference between an individual's unofficial recorded dates and those found when verification is sought. Genealogists prefer to continue to preserve double dates when found in records and label one "o.s." (old style) and the other "n.s." (new style).

♦ 7. A cassette tape recorder with plenty of tapes is quicker than writing, to record information found in libraries and archives. It also may be used in interviews if it does not interfere with the conversation. Some people are microphone shy and will say little when they realize they are being recorded. Tape recordings can provide a personal record of grandparents and great-grandparents for descendants of the future.

♦ 8. If tracing your ancestral roots has led to only a province in Germany -- for example, Hessen, Baden, etc.-- where your immigrant ancestor was born or lived, the state archives of that province may have emigration records that give the village of birth. Locate the address of the archives for the province or state in Germany where you believe your immigrant ancestor lived. Send information listing your ancestor's name, age, names and ages of children born in Germany, everything you know about the family that emigrated and request them to search their emigration lists. If the archives contacted are unable to locate your immigrant ancestor, another possible search may be the German genealogical periodicals having indexes or lists of emigrants for the province you believe you have located.

♦ 9. When all else fails to find the village of your ancestors, search for the same surname in telephone books and lineage books and query people listed who may supply the village of birth of the surname. Many public libraries have a collection of these books. This method may prove to be very discouraging and time consuming, and will test your patience when lack of cooperation exists. However, this problem-solving method has been known to turn into a successful search in difficult genealogical histories.

♦ 10. As a last resort, place ads in genealogical query columns in areas of America and Germany where your ancestors may have lived. This has met with various degrees of success in difficult searches. You may prefer to contact a professional genealogist to work on the problem. Your local library or nearest Genealogical Society assists and directs queries for professional genealogical help. The Family History Library in Salt Lake City and local LDS Family History Centers maintain lists of genealogists who provide research assistance for a fee.

Once the residence locality in Germany of your immigrant ancestor is known, it is well worth your time, expense and effort to plan to continue your search by mail or by travel to Germany for further research and additional discoveries about your family genealogy and heritage. It is impossible to predict in advance the experiences you will encounter, but your viewpoint about your family is bound to expand in the process. First-hand encounters with the German culture in Germany are sure to bring new understandings about the whys and wherefores that influenced your family's values and goals in America. Many of these insights will come at unexpected times and unpredictable events.

After searching by mail I traveled to my native villages in Germany three times to search family genealogy when I discovered that Löhlbach, with a history dating to 800 A.D., was the central village of my ancestry and the village known about in family records in America. In Germany I discovered there were more villages of residence of the family back through the centuries. From the earliest records in Germany the generations of my family lineage could be traced in the Löhlbach parish records. Marriage research revealed family history in ten surrounding lesser-populated villages. This discovery in my first genealogy adventure in Germany was overwhelming. I had not allowed the time or planned to spend enough days in the Löhlbach area to satisfy the needs of that kind of extensive research. The result, a second trip to Germany, was necessary, though not practical for several years.

I learned from my first experience in Germany that tracing genealogy can be more complex and time-demanding than expected once the correct area of emigrant ancestry has been located. I also learned that researchers should not put off plans to trace roots in Germany because it is impossible to predict exactly how much time, effort and finances will be needed to satisfy research interests.

One of my foremost goals in planning the first mail research and travel to Germany to trace the Krug family was to meet anyone still living in my native village who was related to my family. Correspondence with the *Pfarrer* (pastor) of the Löhlbach Church, using only those words for an address, resulted in a reply that no one with the Krug surname lived in the village at that time. However, he did examine the parish records and found recordings of the baptism and confirmation of my great-grandfather, also records of siblings with a notation of the emigration of the family to America in 1865. Accordingly, he confirmed that I had found my "home in Germany." He also confirmed that no one living in the village remembered to the time of the Krug family living in Löhlbach (1865). This did not discourage my enthusiasm in planning to do research and travel in Germany. However, it was not until my third trip to Löhlbach, ten years after my first travel there, that I met for the first time descendants of the Krug family. It took years of searching to locate records of my immigrant Great-Grandfather Krug's aunt, Anna Elisabeth Krug Schüler, the only person with the Krug surname that remained in Löhlbach when her brother and sister-in-law sold their home in the village, and all their possessions, to take their children and sail to America in 1865.

The descendants of Anna Elisabeth Krug Schüler still reside in Löhlbach and surrounding villages and it was a rewarding experience to finally meet these distant paternal cousins.

It was much easier to locate the maternal family lines of my family surname in Germany. Relatives of the wives of the Krug generations are still residents of Löhlbach and surrounding villages. However, due to time constraints, my primary goal in my first mail research and travel to my native village had to be to search the paternal line of my surname, and that became more time-consuming than I expected. When I discovered the parish records were not indexed, I concentrated completely on researching the Krug lineage in the time I had planned to be in Germany. In the process I found my German grandmother's family was from the same village, as were all the great-grandparents on both sides of my Krug family line. I was related to at least six family lines that had roots in Löhlbach and surrounding villages. That is when I realized that it is important to not take on too much research at the same time. Only one surname is enough to research at a time. It is expensive to travel and live in Europe for the length of time it takes to search multiple family lines, therefore, planning research by mail ahead of traveling to Germany is vitally important.

PLANNING RESEARCH IN GERMANY

If you are not planning to hire a professional genealogist to research your family in Germany, it is time to begin preparing to travel to Germany for genealogy research, once the exact location of your native village area has been confirmed via international correspondence. It is important to follow these steps:

♦ STEP ONE: Acquire a map of the German state where your ancestors lived. A *Deutsche Landerkarte* (German landmap) with a scale of 1:250,000 shows all the small villages in rural Germany. It saves many hours of hunting for your native village on maps that do not show the densely populated rural areas of Germany. Without an accurate map of exactly where you will research, it is impossible to make definite plans to search by mail or to journey to the ancestral area.

♦ STEP TWO: The decision to consult an airline directly or visit with a travel agent about an airline and international travel to Germany depends upon whether you plan to have the travel agent make other arrangements for your trip to Europe. You may wish to consult an airline first about the cost of flying to Germany before going ahead with any other plans. It is expensive to buy a roundtrip airline ticket, but well worth the cost when you are learning about yourself and your family's life in the Old Country. If you prefer the assistance of a travel agent, you may phone or stop in for a visit about your plans. Travel agents conveniently sell airline tickets for the same price as airlines offer them for sale.

♦ STEP THREE: Once the decision is made on the time of travel to Germany, plan where you will stay and how many days you will work on family genealogy research. Allow time for making observations of the village area and German countryside other than the time you will actually be working on genealogical records. Notify by correspondence the clergyman of the village(s) you will visit, or nearby villages, and inquire for suggestions for lodging and transportation in the area.

Many of the smaller villages of Germany do not have a church to contact to verify the residence of immigrant ancestors or to make plans with about your first-hand research in the area. In those areas, the nearest church is often the repository of records for the smaller villages. A map of a scale that includes the smaller villages of Germany has symbols marking the villages with churches. Write to the nearest church and inquire about your ancestors. Send an airmail letter giving the full name of your ancestor, the name of the village where they lived, and the date of your ancestor's departure from the village. Also enclose the appropriate number of International Reply Coupons (available at all U.S. Post Offices) for a prompt reply. If that does not bring the desired results, send correspondence addressed to the Rathaus and mayor of the closest city to find clues to the closest records repository where your family records may be located.

♦ STEP FOUR: Once the groundwork has been successfully completed and you have confirmed exactly where, when, and how you plan to travel in Germany, either by rental car, train, or bus to your specific area of research, you are ready to begin thinking about what to take with you for the journey. Hopefully, you will have established person-to-person contact with either a clergyman in the area or a person referred to you who will prove valuable in making suggestions about what you can expect to encounter in your visit.

What the weather will be like, of course, is dependent upon the time of the year travel plans are made. Pack a minimum of clothing using coordinated basic colors in either navy, black or brown.

Comfortable walking shoes are an absolute necessity. Upon arrival in my native village I could not wait to arise early in the morning and walk the streets of the village soon after sunrise to "feel my homeland." Even though I did not know where the streets went, I wandered around the village and was rewarded to find many residents who were early risers, taking care of the livestock that live on the ground level of their fachverk (half-timbered) homes. At an early morning hour, residents had completed their chores with their animals (sheep, cow, pigs) and were leaning on the half-open doors of their ground level barns to watch me walking down the street. It was delightful to call out *"Guten Morgen, Wie Gehts?"* (Good morning. How are you?) as I passed homes. My German words were understood with a cheerful response of the same greeting, only more words were added in Löhlbacher dialect which I could not understand. Even though my part of the conversation was limited, it was an interesting and friendly way to meet the people of the village.

♦ STEP FIVE: Prepare and pack genealogical records and file materials listed earlier in this chapter to include a pedigree chart showing your relationship to the ancestors you are searching. In Germany the pedigree chart will be helpful in explaining your research plans to those who will be assisting with your project in your native village.

RESEARCHING IN GERMANY

One of the joys of researching genealogy in person in Germany is that a Germanic heritage almost always means that traveling in Germany offers a change of culture with a minimum of culture shock. If you are planning to do genealogical research in Northern Germany, it may be convenient to fly to Amsterdam, Holland or Copenhagen, Denmark for travel to Schleswig-Holstein or North Rhineland-Westphalia. The Frankfurt or Berlin airports will be convenient destinations for many other areas of travel in Germany.

Your driver's license will be acceptable for driving a rental car in Europe providing you arrange for use of the car before you leave for Europe. Apply for an International Driver's License if you plan to drive a car in Europe and do not make advance arrangements for doing so before you leave. All highway signs and markers in Germany are written in the German language. If you cannot read German quickly, you need to have a German translator traveling with you in the front seat to read maps and give directions from the signs along the highways. Driving on the continent in Europe is on the same side of the road, keeping to the right, as in the U.S.

In most instances I recommend starting research of your ancestral heritage by first visiting the village known to be where your family lived in the Old Country. You will begin to absorb what it was like for your family to live in Germany before emigrating to the New World. It is easiest to identify and verify your family first in parish records where the family events took place. Some parish records give a column listing the volume number of the civil registry record making it possible to easily find the verification and continued research of places of births, marriages, and deaths in the nearest *Rathaus*. Time is saved by researching parish records first.

On the first visit to my native village I was invited to a wedding in the Löhlbach church where my immigrant Great-Great Grandparents, Johann Justus Krug III and Anna Elisabeth Paar, were married on Christmas Day, 25 December 1835. It is also the church where my Great-Great-Great Grandparents, Johann Justus Krug II and Wilhelmina Kirchner were married 18 May 1804; where Great-Great-Great-Great Grandparents Johann Justus Krug I and Anna Gertrud Möller married 10 May 1763. Additional research in the village of Löhlbach revealed on the maternal side Great-Great Grandmother Anna Elisabeth Paar's parents married in the Löhlbach church 31 March 1807 and her grandparents, Johann Daniel Paar and Katharina Elisabeth Roder married in the same church 2 August 1774. Further Löhlbach research showed Grandmother Christina Happel Krug's grandparents, Andreas Happel and Marie Elisabeth Möller were married in the Löhlbach church 29 May 1843, and her Great-Grandparents, Johann Peter Happel and Anna Gertrud Fackiner married in the Löhlbach church 12 July 1812. Marie Elisabeth Möller's parents, Johannes Möller and Marie Katharina Stremme also married in the Löhlbach church 21 January 1808. An invitation to attend a wedding in the Löhlbach church was a meaningful and nostalgic experience, and one that awakened thoughts about the basic values of my German family's life in America.

The pastor of the Löhlbach church invited me to go with him from the parsonage to the church when the church bells began ringing the length of time required for the bridal party to walk from the bride's home in the village to the church for the ceremony. The pastor stood on the church steps, Bible in hand, with the church door wide open as the bells peeled. I waited in front of the steps listening to the happy sounds of the ringing bells (more than one bell in the belfry ringing at the same time) for what seemed like a long period before the bridal procession came into view in front of the church. There were sixty-five adults and ten children in the bridal party, walking in pairs of two, each man with a woman, the bride and groom leading the procession. The men all dressed in black; some women wore long dresses to the ground, and some wore shorter skirts.

The forty-five minute wedding service was conducted in the German language. At the close of the ceremony, as the bride and groom marched down the aisle, children with baskets full of German coins threw the currency in front of the newly married couple for them to walk over as they exited the church steps. Money rolled all over the sidewalk and down the street. Never before had I seen money thrown and rolling all over, and people walking on money! The pastor explained that throwing money in front of the bride and groom to walk on was traditionally a symbol of good fortune, prosperity, and happiness for the wedded couple. After the bride and groom departed the children scrambled to pick up the coins and pocket them. It was amazing to watch money flying in all directions. German relatives in America valued every coin they had to the extent they carefully dolled out only one coin at a time to children together with an admonishment about how it should be spent and saved. The happiness part of the symbolism of money was easier to understand because my German family often put money and happiness together, though mostly for saving money to have with happiness. In American-German culture it was unthinkable to throw money around, and I could hardly believe my eyes when I saw the large amount of coins thrown and the bride and groom walking on them.

Next, I went to the reception hall to observe the beautiful banquet, the bride and groom cutting their tiered wedding cake, and the large number of deliciously decorated cakes spaced every two to three feet apart along long lines of evenly spaced tables. It was an unforgettable experience.

Every village visit in Germany is rewarded with different experiences. Each is profound and unique in revealing something about the German way of living.

In one ancestral village, a beautifully painted scene on a prominent building of a farmer plowing with Gothic letter inscription, "In farming is the strength of the people" related directly to the values of my German-American Midwestern farming family.

Some experiences of the first-time American genealogy researcher in Germany are totally unexpected and can best be described as a "trip into the past." Reminders of the devastation of war confront a researcher when visiting churches that show reconstruction from World War II bombing. The marvelous restoration of frescoes and friezes is breathtaking. During one of my trips, I saw where the Allied forces crossed the Rhine River while marching to Berlin. Still visible were the initials carved into the tree trunks by the American soldiers liberating Germany in 1945.

On the way to Löhlbach, beside a winding road in central Germany, you can stop along Napoleon's route from Paris to Moscow, which still exists.

The past and the present seem entertwined in Wesel where the Roman Gate in the city square was reconstruction in 1722 and the Roman Empire ruins at Xanten Archaeological Park include a colosseum dated 117 A.D. In a German home, 70- to 100-year-old woven damask draperies still hung beautifully on the windows, and embroidered lines from a Johann von Schiller poem (1759-1805) were visible as lovely fabric shelf-liners with crocheted edging.

It is impossible to travel in Germany without gaining new knowledge, and experiencing cultural viewpoints not previously encountered which have developed during centuries of historic living. Artwork in cathedrals taught Bible stories in the Middle Ages when illiteracy was profuse and printing uninvented. Beautiful three-paneled ("triptych") altars illustrate Bible stories so worshipers visually learn about them. Painted by artists, each scene is depicted in German characters for ease of identification by illiterate worshipers in the process of learning Bible stories. Triptych altars can be observed closely in many Lutheran cathedrals. In the Stadtkirche at Bad Wildungen, the triptych altar of 1403 A.D. (See pages 91, 92) teaches Bible stories showing the earliest known scene of an apostle wearing glasses (p.92), and Joseph cooking food for the Holy Family at the Birth of the Savior (page 92). Counts who lived during the Middle Ages now lie entombed in the cathedral, adding to the historic atmosphere.

It is also impossible to travel among the German people without learning more about the American way of life, and that too comes at unexpected times. *Abendessen* is the evening meal in Germany. I will never forget my feelings at the first invitation to eat sandwiches with a German family at their evening meal of sliced breads, cheeses, meats, and cakes. They served me first and I made a sandwich, then began eating it with my fingers. Their remark, "Oh, that's right! Americans eat with fingers," awakened me to discover Germans make open-faced sandwiches on a plate and eat them bite by bite with a knife and fork. My American way obviously was evidence of a lack of knowledge of table manners in informal living in Germany.

A fun adventure in eating in Germany is trying unfamiliar foods that are steeped in tradition in certain regions. Particularly enjoyable was ordering *Dampfnudeln* with vanilla sauce while traveling in Bavaria. Dampfnudeln must be ordered at least an hour ahead of time because it is a yeast dough shaped in a ball and baked in a cloth to keep it from browning. It is baked after ordering to serve it hot and fresh. The center filling is either plum or prune, and the top covered with vanilla sauce and sprinkled with confectioner's (powdered) sugar. Both a knife and a fork are necessary to eat it.

To fully understand Germany an aesthetic awareness and sensitivity is necessary. The *Luftmaleri* paintings on buildings, Baroque architecture, gold decor and sculpture of palaces, cathedrals, frescoes, friezes, and ciborium altars is indicative of a culture steeped in aesthetic values. Every church has a clock on the tower (some also have clocks on the main altar), and a cock ornament on top of the steeple to symbolize the mortality of man, there is an end to time and man's life, and we are reminded that Peter denied knowing Christ, three times before the cock crowed.

SUMMARY: Determining the exact location where an immigrant was from is very important to being able to research family lineage in Germany. Once in America, many Germans felt they were Americans and no longer German, therefore, they never mentioned where they were from in Germany. When not recorded, clues must be sought by checking sources to determine the place the immigrant came from in Germany. Genealogy homework must be done first to determine the exact place of your ancestors' origin, and thus where to look for civil, parish, and other archive records to verify Germanic roots.

Preparation for researching in Germany, whether by mail or in person, includes planning how, when and where the research will be done. Follow the steps of preparation for a rewarding experience tracing your ancestry and learning about your family in the parish records.

Following pages:

BAD WILDUNGEN STADTKIRCHE 1403 A.D. TRIPTYCH ALTAR: Panel of four paintings (two upper, two lower) on both left and right sides folds into center of altar and covers the crucifixion painting in center. The outsides of the panels are also decorated with religious art. The twelve paintings when the altar is open illustrate the birth and life of Jesus Christ. These picturesn were used to teach the Bible stories in centuries before the Bible was translated into German and most people were illiterate. Details of the paintings of the second picture, upper left, and second from the right, lower right side of the triptych are enlarged on page 92.

TRIPTYCH ALTAR PANELS 1403 A.D.   Bad Wildungen Stadtkirche

BIRTH OF THE SAVIOR

READING APOSTLE

Detail of oldest German art showing use of spectacles

[6]

Genealogical Records and Archives in Germany

What you can expect to find in genealogical records in Germany depends on what has survived the period of wars and historic upheaval in the area you are searching, also how well you have done your homework before beginning research in the Old Country. For most people it is not possible to trace back farther than The Thirty Years' War, 1618-1648. Whole villages, including many churches and parish records, were burned at that time. Only records of the nobility which were privately stored in castles survived those terrible war years.

Before beginning research in Germany you must know:

1. The name of your immigrant ancestor. Do not attempt to search using only a surname before you know who the immigrant ancestor was.

2. In order to find or verify an ancestor's history, you must know about when the birth, marriage or death took place in order to prevent finding another person of the same or similar name, and searching the wrong family line.

3. Since Germany does not have a central records office, it is necessary to know the exact residence of your ancestor at the time of birth, marriage, or death to be sure you are tracing your ancestor and not someone else.

When you have located your immigrant ancestor, tracing your roots in Germany will give you the answer to "Where did I come from?" In the process of searching you will immediately encounter the German language. If you do not read or speak fluent German, do not be discouraged. It will only take longer to decipher the information you are searching. Few Americans are familiar with Gothic lettering and Gothic script. The following section is a practical guide to acquaint you with a beginning understanding of the German language. Since the German language is constantly being modernized in Germany, it is much easier to learn the language when you travel in Europe. Though village people in Germany speak only the German language, it is becoming increasingly possible to find someone in the village who can translate and speak English.

First, familiarize yourself with the German language in printed form. It is easiest if you learn to recognize the Gothic alphabet in both its lower and upper cases (See page 96). Gothic print is unfamiliar to many Americans because feelings toward Germans in the twentieth century were not very good and everything German including Gothic lettering was banished during and after the two World Wars.

All German words used as nouns are capitalized, however, sometimes words are misspelled, nouns are not capitalized, and dialect words and phrases are inserted, making translation more difficult to accomplish. In past centuries grammatical rules were not enforced and many nouns in past records have not been capitalized. Sometimes clergymen writing the records forgot to capitalize proper nouns and names of persons.

Learn to recognize an *umlaut* over a letter -- a diacritical mark of two dots, which designates a change in a vowel and modifies a vowel sound. The German umlaut is used often on letters ä, ö, and ü to represent sounds which do not exist in English. Those vowel sounds can also be written ae, oe, ue. Germans in America often changed the spelling of their surname from having an umlaut in Germany to ae, oe, or ue, for example: Scha(e)ffer, Mo(e)ller or Schu(e)ler.

Another important difference between German and English writing is found in words that have a double "ss" sound. That sound is written in German with this unique symbol -- ß -- which represents two letters of s formed together.

German script has many up and down strokes, often referred to in the agrarian culture of my American birth as "chicken scratching," compared to the oval shapes of English letters. German handwritten letters e, i, u, m, n and sometimes c, when the hook is not put distinctly on it, may all look alike. Training the eye to see alphabet letters in slanted up and down strokes instead of oval shapes is probably the most important technique in learning to read German records. Always look to see if there is an umlaut over any letter, which will be a clue that it is a different vowel sound. However, sometimes it is just an ink spot and a closer inspection of letters is in order. Every writer has their own style of shaping letters, and German script is found written in many ways. Some of the older writing was very decorative (See page 97). The aesthetic designs added to German script make early German writing styles very difficult to decipher. The German script written in 1586 illustrates the difference in earlier writing styles (See page 98).

C is used in German words before the letters h or k, but sometimes in German script the c appears to be absent in the vertical strokes. When using the German pronoun *ich*, meaning "I", the word is not capitalized except at the beginning of a sentence. To translate German script it is best to translate script into the German word first, and then find the English word that has the same meaning, if possible.

Familiarize yourself first with the German script letters that are most like the Latin letters, B, F, I, J, L, O, Z. It is helpful to look for them first when trying to decipher a word. Next, look for the five German script letters which extend high above the line: B, D, K, L, T. It is usually easier to recognize B and L, making it possible to identify the other three letters that extend above the writing line.

Examine the German alphabet to identify the seven letters that extend below the writing line: G, J, P, Q, X, Y, Z. Both J and Z are written similarly in German and Latin lettering. The G, Q, and Y appear to be very similar and often can hardly be distinguished in records. Sometimes the only way to determine which one it is requires remembering that the G is used the most often in words. The Y is often interchanged with the letter I so may be used quite often. Next, notice that the letters P and X also look very much alike. Remembering that P appears more often in words than X may be helpful in translating German to English.

Probably the three letters that are confused the most often are F, H, and S because when written all three have strokes which extend above and below the writing line. Depending upon the style of the writer, all three may look alike and all three letters appear frequently in German script. Of the three letters, the F may be easiest to identify because it is written similar to the Latin alphabet.

The letter S in German script is written in two forms. When S appears within a word it is written with both an up and down stroke. When S appears at the end of a word or syllable it is written in a scroll shape completely above the line. The writing style of the writer may interchange the style of the letter S making it difficult to identify.

In the Schleswig-Holstein area of northern Germany, Danish variations of the German language may be found that date to the time when that area was under Danish rule. Christian I of Denmark inherited Schleswig-Holstein in 1448. From 1864-1920 the area came under German rule, and in 1920 North Schleswig was given back to Denmark.

THE GERMAN GOTHIC SCRIPT

upper case letters
Das große Alphabet.

lower case letters
Das kleine Alphabet.

Early German Script, 1743

TRANSLATION:

Account

of the right honorable prince and Sir Ludwig, Landgrave of Hessen, prince of Hersfeld, count of Katzenelenbogen, Dietz, Ziegenhain, Nidda, Schaumburg, Isenburg and Büdingen concerning my most gracious prince's and master's annual rents and income of money, fruit, poultry and other things of the castle, town and magistracy of Biedenkopf. Begun January 1st and closed the last of December 1743.

Performed by me, the princely bailiff
Caspar Christian Teüthorn

Early German Script, 1586

TRANSLATION:

Register of real property and inheritance of His serene Highness and Right honorable prince and master, Sir Ludwig Langrave of Hessen, Count of Katenallenboden, Dietz, Ziegenhain and Nidda, of our gracious prince, master of Blankenstein, his magnificence and justice, jurisdiction, penal law, command, taxes and rates and other profits and property by us, the treasurers of Blankenstein and the registrars, as well as the mayors and troopers of Gladenbach, Wolf Heinzenberger, Echard Scholer, Joachim Wetter and Otto Wagenbach on the report of the chairmen and the eldest and most experienced of the magistracy, as well as from old registers, written documents and preformed according to the common usage.

In the year of 1586

GERMAN TERMINOLOGY

To read Gothic script and understand German words it is helpful to have a basic knowledge of commonly used words and phrases in genealogy recordings. The different sections of Germany adhered to variations of spelling until the twentieth century, therefore, genealogy research discloses archaic dialect usage of words. The various German speaking groups of Europe, such as the Swabians, Saxons, Austrians, and Swiss can each be distinguished by the pronunciation peculiar to speaking their native dialects.

German nouns are capitalized and have gender prefixes: *der* (male), *die* (female), and *das* (neuter). Sometimes adjectives may be capitalized. Many words are spelled almost the same as in English though they may differ considerably in pronunciation. In German pronunciation, the principle stress is on the root syllable (usually the first one), but every syllable is pronounced distinctly. Careful listening may make it possible to increase your German vocabulary after studying this word list.

Abend = evening
Ackermann = farmer, husband-man
Adel = noble, nobility
adelig = nobleman, of nobility
adoptiert = adopted
Adresse = address
Akt = act
Alkohol = alcohol
Alphabet = alphabet
Alt = old
am fogenden Tage = on the following day
am gleichen Tage = on the same day
Anekdote = anecdote
Appetit = appetite
auf = on, upon, at
aus = out, out of, from, of
Ausfahrt = exit
Auswanderung = emigration
Automobil = automobile

Ball = ball
Bank = bank
Bauer = peasant

Bauern = farmer
beerdigt = buried
beerd.tag = burial date
begraben = buried
Berg = mountain, hill
Bergmann = miner
Bett = bed
Bier = beer
Block = block
Blong = blond
Bruder = brother
Buch = book
Burg = castle
Burgerregistrieren = citizen register
Butter = butter

Christkind = infant Jesus
circa = about, approximately

diagonal = diagonal
Differenz = difference
direckt = direct
Doktor = doctor
Dorf = village

Ehe = marriage
Ehebrucher = adulterer
Ehegatte = husband
Ehefrau = wife
Einwanderer = immigrant
Einwanderung = immigration
Ende = end
Eltern = parents
Enkel = grandson
Enkelin = granddaughter
evangelisch = Evangelical
extra = extra
Export = export

Familie = family
Familiename = surname
Familiengeschichte = genealogy
Forster = forester
Frau = wife, woman
Frucht = fruit

geboren = born
Geburt = birth
Geburtsbrief = birth certificate
Geburtsschein = birth certificate
Gemeinde = community
geschieden = divorced
Geschlecht = sex, gender
Geschwister = siblings
gestern = yesterday
gestorben = died
getauft = baptized
getraut = married
Gott = God
Graf = count
Grosseltern = grandparents
Grossmutter = grandmother
Grossvater = grandfather

haben = have
Hand = hand
Haus = house
Hause, zu = at home
Hebamme = midwife

heirat = marriage/ *Heirath* (old form)
heiraten = to marry
Hinterbliebene = survivor
Hunger = hunger

im = in the
instruktion = instruction

Jahr = year
Jahrestag = anniversary
Jungfrau = virgin, unmarried
Junggeselle = bachelor
Junggesellin = bachelor girl

Katholisch = Catholic
Katholische Kirche = Catholic Church
Kaufmann = merchant, businessman
Kind = child
Kinder = children
Kirche = church
Kirchenbuch = parish book
Klasse = class
Knabe = boy
Konfirmation = confirmation
Konversation = conversation
Krankheit = sickness, disease
Kreis = district
Küfer = cooper

Land = land
Landsiedler = settler
Leben = life
Lebend = living
ledig = single, unmarried
Leichen = funeral
Leinweber = linenweaver
letzter Wille = last will

Madchen = girl
Mann = man, husband
Maurer = mason

Metzger = butcher
Monat = month

morgen = tomorrow
Muller = miller
Mutter = mother

nach = after, to, according
Nachmittag = afternoon
Nacht = night
Name = name
Nation = nation
Neffe = nephew
Neujahr = new year

Ober = upper, above
Onkel = uncle
Ort = place, village, town
Ostern = Easter
Ostermontag = Easter Monday

Pate = godfather, godchild
Pfarrbuch = parish book
Pfarrhaus = parsonage
Pfarrer = minister, pastor
Platz = place
Priester = priest

Rathaus = city hall
Reformierte Kirche = Reformed Church
Rentner = retired person

Schafer = shepherd
Schloss = castle
Schmied = blacksmith
Schneider = tailor
Schuhmacher = shoemaker
Schule = school
Schullehrer = school teacher
Schuster = shoemaker
Schreiber = writer
Schwagerin = sister-in-law
schwanger = pregnant
Schwester = sister

Schwiegermutter = mother-in-law
Schwiegersohn = son-in-law
Schwiegervater = father-in-law
Seite = book page
sepultus (Latin) = buried
Schreiner = cabinetmaker, joiner
Sohn = son
Soldat = soldier
Sohner = Daughter-in-law
sohnlein = little son
sponso (Latin) = to marry
Staat = state
Stadt = city
Standesamt = registry office
sterben = to die
Steuerbuch = tax register
Stiefkind = stepchild
Steifmutter = stepmother
Stiefsohn = stepson
Stiefvater = stepfather
Strasse = street

Tag = day
Tagelohner = day laborer
Tante = aunt
Taufe = baptism
Taufbuch = baptismal register
Taufpaten = godparents
Taufzeugen = baptism witnesses
Telefon = telephone
Tochter = daughter
Tochterlein = little daughter
Tod = death
Todesursache = cause of death
Todestag = death date
tot = dead
todtgeboren = stillborn
Trauung = marriage

unbestimmte Krankheit = undefined illness
unehelich = illegitimate
unter = lower, under, below
Unterleibstyphus = Typhoid fever
Urenkel = grandson

Urgrossmutter = great-grand-
mother
Urgrossvater = great-grandfather
Urkunde = document

Vater = father
verloben = become engaged
Verlobte, der = bridegroom
Verlobte, die = bride
Verlobung = engagement, be-
throthal
vermahlt = married
verheirathet = married (old form)
verstorben = deceased
Verzeichnis = register
Vetter = male cousin
Volkszahlung = census
von = of, from
Vorfahr = ancestor
Vormund = guardian
Vorname = Christian name
Vorn.Eheg = male first name
Vorn.Mu = mother's Christian
name

Vorn.Va = father's Christian
name

Waise, die = orphan
werden = to become
wieder = again
Witwe = widow
Witwer = widower
wohnen = to live
wurde geboren = was born
wurde getauft = was baptized
wurden = were

Zeit = time
Zeit der Geburt = time of birth
Zeuge = witness
Zimmermann = carpenter
Zimmermeister = master carpen-
ter
Zivilstandsamt = civil registrar's
office
Zuname = surname
Zwillinge = twins

The German language has a basic vocabulary of politeness. It is a good idea when writing to Germany, or when traveling there to often use the words *bitte* (please) and *danke* (thank you). There are formal and informal manners of addressing a person in Germany. If a person is unknown, a formal greeting using *Sie* is appropriate. An informal greeting using *du* is a sign of familiarity, friendliness or affection. Practicing the German alphabet out loud helps in learning the pronunciation of German words:

The German Alphabet

a - *ah*	n - *enn*
b - *bay*	o - *oh*
c - *tseh*	p - *pay*
d - *day*	q - *ku*
e - *ay*	r - *air*
f - *eff*	s - *ess*
g - *gay*	t - *tay*
h - *hah*	u - *oo*
i - *ee*	v - *fau*
j - *yot*	w - *vay*
k - *kah*	x - *iks*
l - *ell*	y - *upsilon*
m - *emm*	z - *tset*

Numbers	Days of the Week	Months
eins - one	*Montag* - Monday	*Januar* - January
zwei - two	*Dienstag* - Tuesday	*Februar* - February
drei - three	*Mittwoch* - Wednesday	*Marz* - March
vier - four	*Donnerstag* - Thursday	*April* - April
funf - five	*Freitag* - Friday	*Mai* - May
sechs - six	*Samstag* - Saturday	*Juni* - June
sieben - seven	*Sontag* - Sunday	*Juli* - July
acht - eight		*August* - August
neun - nine		*September* - September
zehn - ten		*Oktober* - October
		November - November
		Dezember - December

Norden - North
Suden - South
Osten - East
Westen - West

When asking a question in the German language, reverse the word order:

Lernen Sie? Are you learning? (*Sie* = formal form of "you")
Lerne ich? Do I learn?
Lernst du? Do you learn? (*du* = informal form of "you")
Lernt er? Does he learn?
Lernt sie? Does she learn?
Lernen wir? Do we learn?
Lernen sie? Do they learn?

When asking a question in the negative form, reverse the word order and use the negative *nicht*:

Lerne ich nicht? Don't I learn?
Lernst du nicht? Don't you learn?
Lernt er nicht? Doesn't he learn?
Lernt sie nicht? Doesn't she learn?
Lernen wir nicht? Don't we learn?
Lernen sie nicht? Don't they learn?

Sentences that help in German:

Guten Morgen! Hello! Good morning.
Guten Abend. Good night.
Sehr gut. Very well.
Sehr gut, danke. Very well, thanks.
Wiederholen Sie, bitte. Please repeat.

Wie geht est Ihnen? How are you?

Sprechen Sie Deutsch? Do you speak German?

Nein, ich spreche nicht Deutsch. No, I don't speak German.

Ich spreche nicht gut Deutsch. I don't speak German very well.

Ja, ich spreche ein wenig. Yes, I speak a little.

Verstehen Sie? Do you understand?

Nein, ich verstehe nicht. No, I don't understand.

Wurden Sie langsam sprechen, kann ich Sie verstehen? Would you please say that again? (Would you repeat that, please?)

Wenn Sie langsam sprechen, kann ich Sie verstehen. If you speak slowly, I can understand you.

Ja, ich verstehe ein wenig. Yes, I understand a little.

Ich lese, aber ich kann nicht sprechen. I read but can't speak.

Verstehen Sie? Do you understand?

Bitte, sprechen Sie langsam. Please speak slowly.

Ich verstehe Deutsch nich sehr gut. I don't understand German very well.

Wie schreiben Sie es? How do you write (spell) it?

Ich kenne das Wort nicht. I don't know that word.

Bitte schon. You're welcome, or Please (nicely).

Bitte sehr. Certainly, or Thank you very much.

Wie bitte? Pardon. What did you say?

Bis heute Abend. See you this evening. (Until this evening.)

Auf Wiedersehen! Good-bye. See you soon.

Grüs Gott. (Hello in south Germany.) Greetings to God.

Fachverk and Slate Löhlbach Kirche

PARISH REGISTERS

When your ancestral village in Germany is known, you can use the *Kirchenbucher* (parish register books) from Germany to trace your family lineage. The major churches of Germany -- Lutheran, Reformed, and Catholic -- kept excellent records and almost all Germans belonged to one of the major state-supported churches. To research your German ancestry you need to know if your immigrant ancestor was Protestant or Catholic. Few villages have more than two denominations - Roman Catholic and Protestant. The Protestants are either Lutheran, Evangelical or Reformed. Most villages were predominatly of one religion. Northern Germany is predominantly Protestant; Southern Germany is mainly Catholic. Smaller sects did not keep records, to prevent exposure to persecution.

Whether or not a family attended church regularly, all children were baptized as infants, many on the day they were born; all marriages were performed in church; and all people were buried by the church. A village parish served a number of areas where homes were grouped together called *Hof* (farms).

Stadt = city   Dorf = village
Hof = farm homes
Muhle = Mill

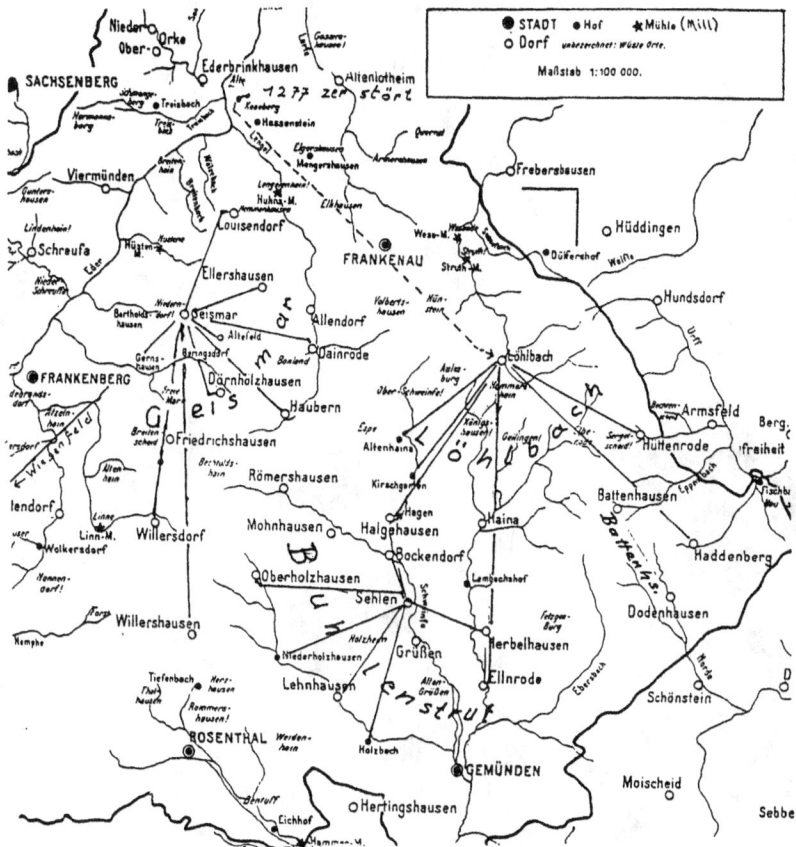

Map of communities served by churches
at Geismar, Löhlbach, and Sehlen

_[107]_

VILLAGE OF BATTENHAUSEN

Parish records are primary sources where you will find information about your ancestors. They begin about 1550 and are located either at the local parish office (*Pfarramt*) or with the bishop of the diocese. See Löhlbach Parish Register Book:

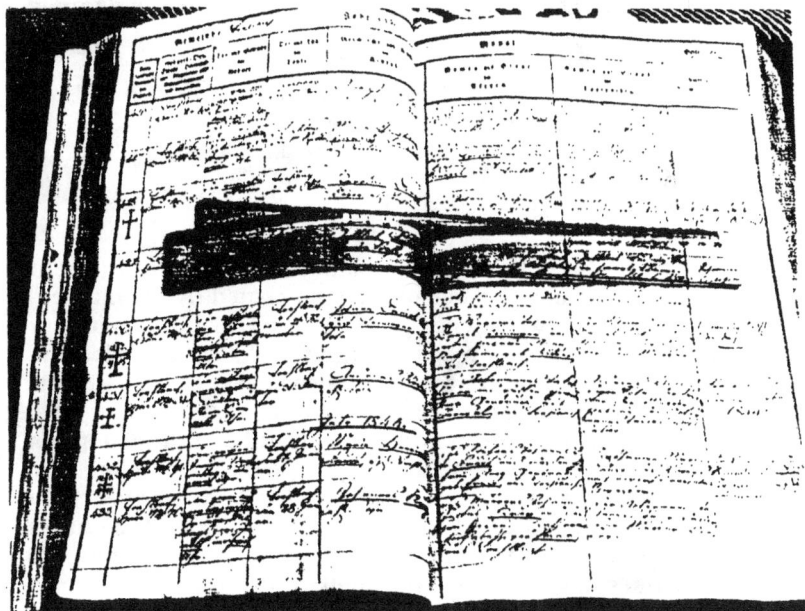

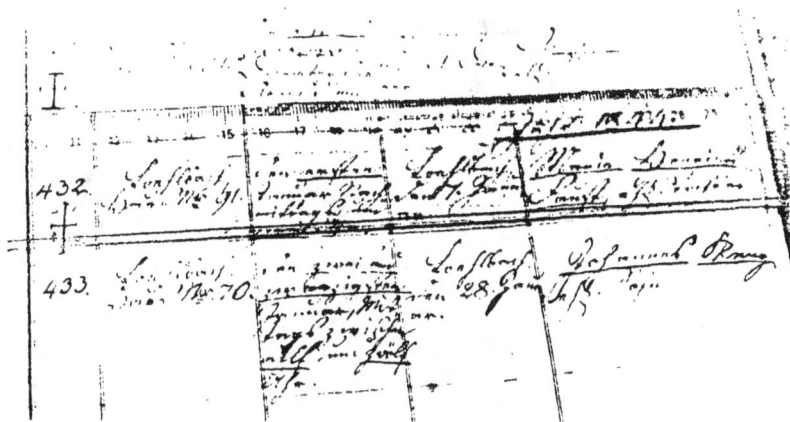

Taufregister for 1844 showing #433
Johann Peter Krug, House Nr. 70 Löhlbach

Records kept by the clergy of the church include baptisms, confirmations, marriages, and burials. In some areas the *Kirchenbucher* from several parishes are gathered together at an archive called *Kirchenbuchamter.* See page 112 for a family pedigree extracted from parish records, and page 113 for Kirchenbucher research of a family line during the Nazi years.

The address of the genealogical institution for research of East Prussian Members of Evangelical Church is:
Evangelische Kirche der Union Kirchenkanzlei
Jebenstra. 3
W 1000 Berlin 12

The monks at Haina Kloster kept elaborate records of the rent that was paid by farmers for use of the land owned by the church. For centuries the land was owned by either the Duke of the area or by the church. Krug family research into the 1600's revealed the number of sheaves of grain the family paid each year to Haina Kloster as rent for farming the land (See page 116).

In the seventeenth, eighteenth, and nineteenth centuries infants were usually baptized the same day they were born, therefore, the parish register records their baptism, and in some instances a mention of birth date. Most baptismal registers contain the child's name and baptism, the father's status and occupation, the family's residence, names of godparents and their relationship to the baptized child, and the mother's maiden name.

Names will be spelled the way the parish clergy spelled the name. With new clergy sometimes there was a new spelling of names. Thus, if a family moved to a different village, their name may have a different spelling. For example, Frederick Fischer in one village may be spelled Friedrik Fisher in another village. Some clergymen were better writers than others, and it is sometimes difficult to decipher the handwriting in parish registers to correctly identify relatives' names. The capital letters K and R have a similar look in German script. If you are aware of this similarity, it may save you years of searching in the wrong parish records.

Parish registers in the seventeenth and eighteenth centuries were often written in Latin and are difficult to read because of a combination of German and Latin words in the same sentences, complicating grammatical translation (See pages 117, 119). *Anno* is the Latin word for year, as illustrated on page 117 dated 1692 and 1693 and written with a quill. The third item recorded under 1693: Altenhaina marriage of Great- Great- Great- Great- Great- Great- Grandfather Johann Krug 18 May, 1693 to Maria Elisabeth Konrad, widow of Bornschier (Bornscheur) married at Bodenhausen.

The Latin baptism register for 1696 (See page 119) reads: 23 April Johann Jost Krug's small son Johann Hartman baptized at Altenhaina; his godfather was a brother-in-law from Herbelhausen. The heading on page 121, *Catalogus Sepultorum*, is Latin for Catalogue of Burials. Recorded: 28 February 1736 Altenhaina burial of Maria Elisabeth, widow of Johann Krug, daughter of Krausshaar, miller at Bringshausen, born 1664, married 1684, Jan 22nd to Conrad Bornschier. Two sons and two daughters. Her husband was slain by a shepherd from Haddeburg, second marriage 1693 to Johann Just Krug. Two sons and three daughters.

Latin was widely used by clergy, especially in Catholic records, but Protestant ministers also used the ancient language. Some pastors made up their own forms of Latin, therefore, words used by ecclesiastics between 1500 and 1880 are not standard spellings. The clergy and priests were sometimes not expert in handling the two languages, adding to the difficulty, and some words are now archaic in the German language. It takes an experienced genealogy researcher to decipher the meaning of the sentences.

It is a challenge to the aspiring genealogist to learn enough of the German language to be able to translate information once the parish records pertaining to ancestors have been found. Many genealogists develop enough skills to do this. Inexpensive bilingual dictionaries are available and are useful tools to assist in the learning process. Learn as much as possible about the language and expressions used in the records that tell about your German people. Terms that refer to feast days, occupations, geographical expressions, abbreviations, former political expressions, and Latin forms for expressions and localities are a constant challenge to the genealogy researcher in Germany (See pages 99-105).

The Löhlbach parish death register for 1778, page 122, translates "between Dec 18 and 24th Anna Gertrud, wife of Johann Just Krug, born 1735 at Halgenhausen, daughter of Johannes Mollner and Anna Gertrud nee Wilhelmi, confirmed at Mohnhausen in 1748, married 1763 on May 10th, four sons and two daughters, died in confinement, as she had given birth to a premature daughter, who was baptized at once and given the name of Anna Gertrud, but who died right after being baptized."

Many parish registers in Germany have been microfilmed by the Mormon Church and are available through any local Family History Center of the LDS.

The naming of children in German families was culturally defined with Biblical names. A favorite Bible name for boys was: John (spelled *Johann* or *Johannes* in German language). Other common names for boys were Heinrich, Wilhelm, and Friedrich. In many families the first names of both father and mother were given to

Familienkundliche Zeichen:
* = geboren
~ = getauft (auch †)
⋈ = vermählt (auch ∞)
II.⋈ = 2. Ehe
+ = gestorben, ⚔ = gefallen
☐ = beerdigt (auch †)

Johann Justus
Krug
Löhlbach (Haus № 70)

Johann Justus Krug
Löhlbach
* 16. September 1725
+ 4. April 1786

Johann Justus
Krug
Löhlbach (Haus № 70)
Germany

* ~ 18 Mai 1775
+ ☐ 9 April 1847

⋈ II 10 Mai 1763
Anna Gertrud Möller
Halgehausen
* ~ 1735
+ ☐ 18. Dezember 1775

× 18 Mai 1804
Löhlbach

Ludwig Kirchner
Schwabendorf
*
+ ☐

Wilhelmina Kirchner
Schwabendorf
* ~ 18. Nov. 1805
+ ☐

* ~ 1767
Schwabendorf
+ ☐ 22. Nov. 1855
Löhlbach

×
Marie Madeline Badonin
Schwabendorf
* ~
+ ☐

Johann Peter
Krug
Löhlbach (№ 70)
Germany

* ~ 22 Januar 1844
+ ☐

× 25. Dezember 1835
Löhlbach

Johannes Paar
Löhlbach (Haus № 10)

Johann Daniel Paar
Löhlbach (Haus № 10)
* 30. März 1736
+ 14. Juni 1819

Anna Elisabeth
Paar
Löhlbach (Haus № 10)
* ~ 16. März 1811

* ~ 20 Oktober 1789
+ ☐ 4. Januar 1856
Löhlbach

× 2. August 1774
Kath. Elisabeth Röder
Löhlbach
* ~ 11. März 1750
+ ☐ 14. Nov. 1808

× 31 März 1807
Löhlbach

+ ☐

Anna Elisab. Prächter
Allenhaina - Germany
* ~ 3 Januar 1786
+ ☐ 19 Februar 1814
Löhlbach

Johann Peter Prächter
Allenhaina
* ~ 11 Januar 1763
+ ☐ 11 Februar 1836

× 13 Januar 1785
Anna Katharina Ochse
Halgehausen
* ~ 6. Januar 1763
+ ☐ 25. September 1825

Quellen: Kirchen bücher
Löhlbach

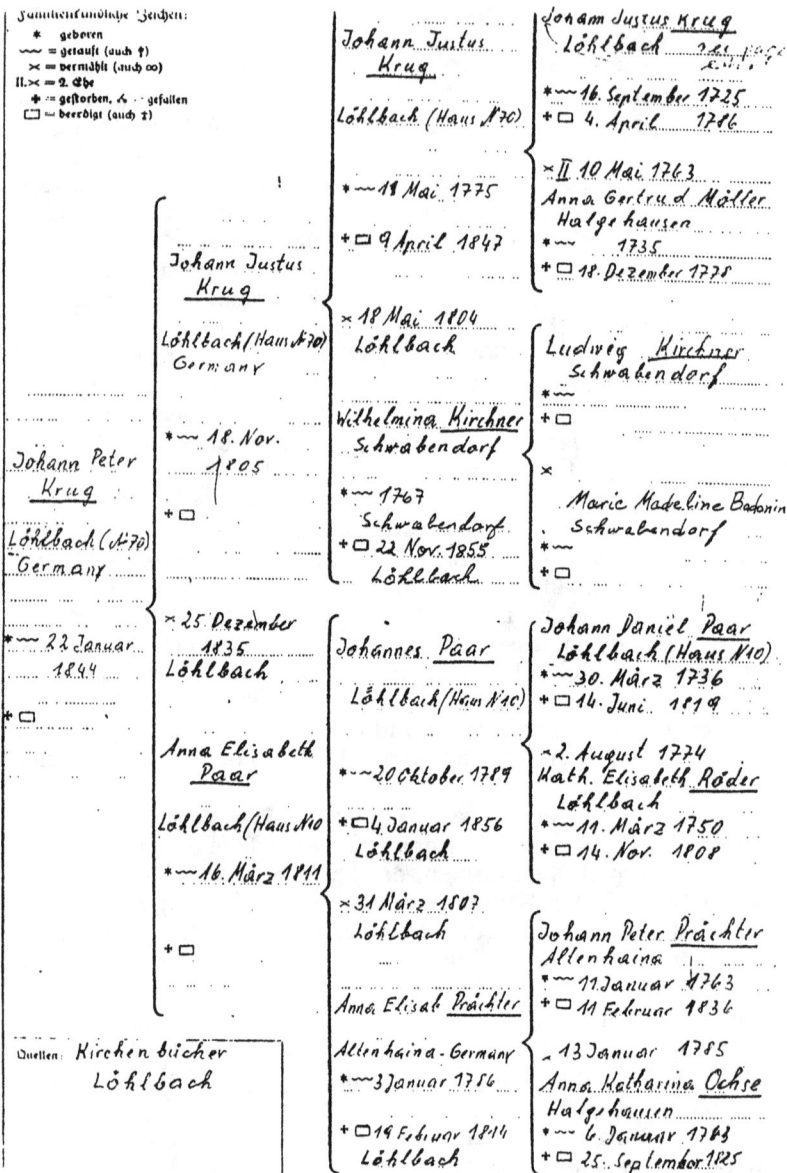

Family pedigree extracted from parish records

[112]

Auszug aus den Kirchenbüchern der evgl. Pfarrei Lißberg

(Nur gültig für die Zwecke des rechtlichen Abstammungsnachweises.)

Friedrich Wilhelm
Möller
geb. in Lißberg
am 25.3.1881
getauft in Lißberg
am 10.4.1881
getraut in
am
gestorben in
am

Ahnennummer

Wilhelm Möller	Marie Karoline Landau
geb. in Lißberg	geb. in Lißberg
am 23.3.1843	am 7.5.1849
getauft in Lißberg	getauft in Lißberg
am 2.4.1843	am 13.5.1849
getraut in Lißberg	
am 18.4.1870	
gestorben in Lißberg	gestorben in Lißberg
am 7.1.1893	am 22.3.1929

Ahnennummer u. Ahnenvermerk

Balthasar Möller	Anna Elisabeth Jäger	Johann Jakob Landau	Anna Elisabeth Graß
geb. in Lißberg	geb. in Römershausen	geb. in Lißberg	geb. in Lißberg
am 29.1.1808	am 9.3.1809	am 6.9.1820	am 23.8.1824
getauft in Lißberg	getauft in Römershausen	getauft in Lißberg	getauft in Lißberg
am 31.1.1808	am	am 7.9.1820	am 29.8.1824
getraut in Lißberg		getraut in Lißberg	
am 23.4.1832		am 9.11.1845	
gestorben in Lißberg	gestorben in Lißberg	gestorben in Lißberg	gestorben in Lißberg
am 7.11.1875	am 13.1.1874	am 17.4.1897	am 14.5.1892

Ahnennummer		Ahnennummer		Ahnennummer		Ahnennummer	
Lukas Möller	Anna Elisabeth Jäger	Johann Heinrich Jäger	Anna Marie Müller	Johann Konrad Landau	Marie Karoline Weigel	Johann Adam Graß	Anna Marie Möller

für die Richtigkeit: Lißberg, den 26.8. 1936

(Siegel: Evangelisches Pfarramt Lißberg in Hessen)

W. Möller, Pfr.

Nachdruck verboten.
Wilh. Dißmeyer, Gyle bei Bremen.

Kirchenbucher research of a family line during Nazi years

children, often to the firstborn son and daughter, and many grand-parents' names were passed along. Aunts, uncles and grandparents automatically gave their names to the infant when they were baptismal sponsors. From the early seventeenth century to the mid-nineteenth century, families tended to use necronyms - the names of deceased siblings.

German families preferred to name their daughters after Christian saints: Elisabeth, Katharina, Margaretha, Anna, and Maria were favorites. Sons were named after Frankish knights and kings: Frederick, Wilhelm, Karl, August, George, and Heinrich.

Parish registers contain much of the same information as the civil registry office records. If there is a difference, it is that baptism or christening dates are given instead of actual birth dates. Sometimes both dates are listed in parish records (see page 120, Kirburg parish baptism records for 1881 and 1882), but more often only the date of baptism is recorded due to the fact that in earlier years babies were baptized the same day they were born. Parish registers are quite specific in noting illegitimacy. Stillborn babies, and infants that died unbaptized, were not entered in birth registers, but appear in death registers.

Parish marriage records often give information about the age or parentage of the bride and bridegroom and the number of the house of residence in the village.

Parish burial records give the age at death in years, months, and days, making it possible to determine actual birth date. For example, if a person died 21 Oct 1879, age 69 years, 8 months, 14 days, the actual birthdate is 7 February 1810. Parish confirmation records also verify birthdate or age of the person, however, if the actual year of birth is not known, or is inaccurate, it is difficult to locate the confirmation record, also recorded by year due to the usual lack of indexing of parish records. Information found in parish records:

TAUFREGISTER - BAPTISM or CHRISTENING REGISTER
    The date of baptism; date of birth (listed in some parish records)
    The name of child;
    The sex;
    The name, surname, residence, religion of the father;
    The name, surname, maiden name, residence, religion of mother;
    The rank, profession or occupation of the father;
    The name(s) and residence of baptismal sponsors/ godparents;
    The relationship of sponsors/ godparents to the child.
    The civil register number recording of birth (in some parish records).

Stillborn or unbaptized babies appear only in parish death registers.

TRAUREGISTER - MARRIAGE REGISTER
  The date of wedding;
  The names, surnames, dates of birth, residences, and religion of persons marrying;
  The condition (widow, widower, etc.);
  Their rank, profession or occupation;
  The name, surname, profession or occupation of the fathers (listed in some parish records);
  Dates of announcement of forthcoming marriage (in some parish records);
  The civil register number recording the marriage (in some parish records).

Widows used the surnames of their deceased husbands, and researchers must search for records of her first marriage in order to determine the maiden surname of brides in second marriages.

BEGRABENEN REGISTER - BURIAL REGISTER
  The date and place of burial;
  The time of burial (in some parish records);
  The name and surname of the deceased;
  The sex of the deceased;
  The age at burial;
  The rank, profession or occupation of deceased;
  The civil death register number (in some records).
  The cause of death may be given under remarks.
  Upper class Lutherans about 1550-1800 printed and distributed funeral sermons, accounts of life of deceased, listings of names of relatives and ancestors.

OTHER CHURCH RECORDS - Confirmation (*Konfirmationsregister*), communion, and confession lists, family registers (See page 109), and penances (*Kirchenstrafen*).
  Protestant records begin earlier in Germany than Catholic records. Records for religious groups other then Lutheran, Reformed and Catholic are mostly fragmentary.

Symbols used in Parish Registers:

  *   = *Geboren* - born
  〜〜 = *Getauft* - baptized
  ✕   = *Vermahlt* - married
  +   = *Gestorben* - died
  ⬓   = *Begraben* - Burial

Haina Kloster Records of the 1600's.
Librarian is pointing to Krug entry of sheaves of grain paid
to the church for use of farmland.

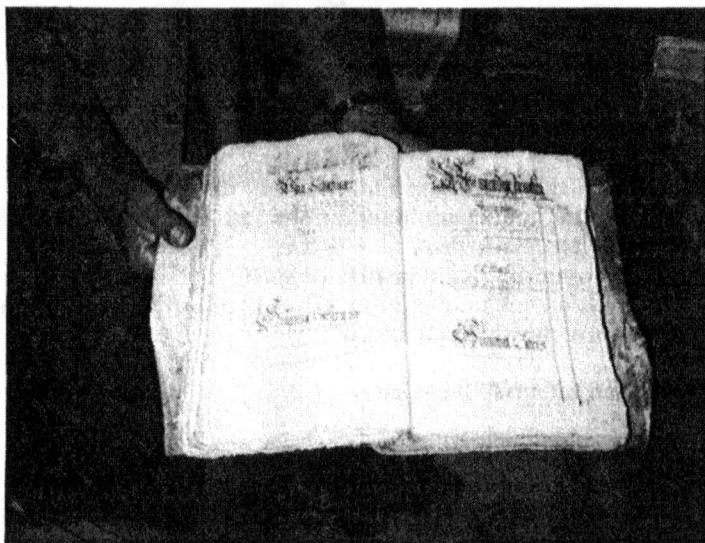

1600's Haina Kloster Records showing
elaborate designs inscribed on each page.

Löhlbach Parish Latin Marriage Register, 1692-1693: *Note: Use of Latin with German script. "1693 - 18 May Johann Jost Krug and Maria Elixabeth Konrad, widow of Bornshier (Bornscheur?) were married at Bodenhausen."

KIRBURG PARISH MARRIAGE REGISTER 1880

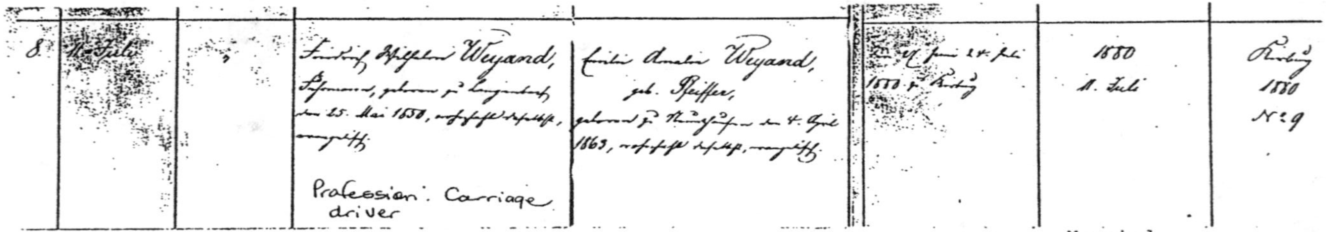

8

11 July

Friedrich Wilhelm Weyand,
carriage driver, born in
Langenbach 25 May 1850
marriage Lutheran

Profession: Carriage
driver

Emilie Amalia Weyand,
born Pfeiffer,
born Neunkhausen 4 April
1863, Lutheran

Announced
27 June-4 July
1880 at Kirburg

Married
1880
11 July

Kirburg
1880
Regist.
No.9

Löhlbach Parish Latin Baptism Register 1696: "April 23 Johann Jost
Krug's small son Johann Hartman baptized at Altenhaina, Godfather
has become a brother-in-law from Herbelhausen."
*Note: Use of Latin with German script.

KIRBURG PARISH BAPTISM REGISTER 1881 & 1882

Tag der Taufe.	Des Getauften		Name, Stand, Geburts-Wohnort und Confession		Ort		Führungsort, Jahrgang, Nummer des bürgerlichen Geburts-Registers	Jahr und Tag der Geburt.
	Taufname.	Familienname.	des Vaters.	der Mutter.				
# Day of Baptism	Baptized Name	Family Name	Father	Mother	Place	Godparents	Born Kirburg	
5 June	Richard	Weyand	Friedrich Weyand, born Neunkhausen Lutheran	Emilie Amalia born Pfeiffer Neunkhausen Lutheran		Neunkhausen	All from Langenbach Heinrich Weyand 19 Augusta Gross Elisa Ramy	1881 #26 May 1881 19 Mai 1881 Birth-date N:9
						Sponsors (1) Elisabeth Weyand (2) Heinrich Weyand (3) Elisa Ramy, Augusta Gross		

Second Child born to parents in 1882 register:

*note Nr. 61 Civil Registry (See on page ____)

(Not of Sponsors)

Kirburg Parish Baptism Register 1881 & 1882

Löhlbach Parish Latin Burial Register. *Note: Use of Latin with German script. "1736 Altenhaina, 28 February Maria Elisabeth, widow of Johann Krug, daughter of Krasshaar, miller at Brinkhausen, born 1664, married 1684, 22 January to Conran Bornschier, two sons and two daughters. Her husband was slain by a shepherd from Haddeburg, second marriage 1693 to Johann Jost Krug. Two sons and three daughters."

Löhlbach Parish Latin Burial Register 1778-1779. *Note: Use of Latin with German script. "Anna Gertrud, wife of Johann Justus Krug, born 1735 at Halgehausen, daughter of Johannes Möller and Anna Gertrud née Wilhelmi, confirmed at Mohnhausen in 1748, married 1763 on May 10th, four sons and two daughters, died in confinement, as she had given birth to a premature daughter, who was baptized at once and given name Anna Gertrud but who died right after being baptized."

DAY	PLACE	NAME, POSITION, BIRTH, DOMICILE, CONFESSION
OF BURIAL		AT BURIAL	Age at Burial

7	Kirburg	Weyand, Richard second son	born 31 March 1887
Feb.		born 31 March 1881.	died 5 February 1889
		Lutheran	age 1 year, 10 months, 5 days

Berzeichn der Begrabenen.

Tag des Begräbnisses.	Ort des Begräbnisses.	Name, Stand, Geburts-, Wohnort und Conf. der Begrabenen.	Alter des Begrabenen.	Führungsort, Zuhgang und Nummer des bürgerlichen Civil-Registers	Bemerkung
7. Februar.	Kirburg.	Weyand, *[handwritten]*	*[handwritten]*	Kirburg, 1889, N 8.	*[handwritten]* Died of Scarlet Fever

[123]

CIVIL REGISTRATION AND ARCHIVE RECORDS

Tracing records in Germany can be more complex than in America, depending upon the individual family circumstances and the location of family roots in Germany. The sources available for research depend upon the history over the centuries of the area you wish to search. There is no one answer to where the records repositories are in Germany. You must search for answers to where records are kept in the particular location of the origin of your ancestor's birth or place of residence to uncover clues to the type of records that exist. The place of residence often is a village other than where parish and civil records were kept.

German states began officially recording births, marriages, and deaths in different years. In 1849 recordings began regardless of religion. Previously persons of different religious confessions did not marry because the Roman Catholic Church and Protestant denominations did not permit mixed marriages.

If your search is in an area that was heavily bombed during World War II, all civil records may have been destroyed. If that is the case, then parish records may be the only available primary sources to trace your ancestors. This was the situation I found in Kassel, Germany, an industrial city in World War II, heavily bombed with all civil records destroyed. Civil registry in Kassel, Hessen-Nassau, began in 1803. The parish registers at Löhlbach, near Kassel, contained records dating to the sixteenth century, making it possible to trace my Krug family back through the generations.

Records may also be found in either city or state archives depending upon the locale you are researching. In sections of Germany where records have been destroyed by fire, lost, or damaged by war, tracing family history may be a time-consuming search through church, government, state and land, city and district, university, or occupation archives. Libraries, museums, and civil authorities can be contacted for clues to information that will lead to records repositories helpful in determining ancestral history.

The *Standesamtbezirke* (Vital Records Registration District) encompasses more than one *Gemeinden* (community or township) without consideration to ancient parish boundaries. Sometimes it is easier to find marriage records after 1849 here, than to try to locate them in a parish register.

An 1875 law made civil registration mandatory in Germany. Beginning January 1, 1876, local registry offices (*Standesamt* in the German language) were established throughout Germany to record births, marriages, and deaths regardless of faith and religion. Every province in Germany also has its state archives (*Staatsarchiv* in German language) where civil vital records are kept, but most of these do not begin until the nineteenth century. Civil vital records may also be found in municipal archives (*Stadtsarchiv*) or national archives (*Hauptstaatsarchiv*).

Civil registry in German states (English name in parenthesis) began as follows:

Schleswig-Holstein - 1874
Mecklenburg - 1876
Brandenburg - 1874
Niedersachsen (Lower Saxony) - 1809
Saxon-Anhalt - 1850-1874
Nordrheim Westfalen (North Rhine-Westphalia) - 1808
Hessen (Hesse) - 1803
Thuringen (Thuringia) - 1876
Sachsen (Saxony) - 1876
Rheinland-Pfalz (Rhineland-Palatinate) - 1792
Saarland (Saar) - 1792
Baden-Wurttemberg - 1876
Bayern (Bavaria) - 1876

The latest editions (See Bibliography, page 147) of Thomas Jay Kemp's *International Vital Records Handbook* and Ernest Thode's *The Address Book for Germanic Genealogy*, available in many public libraries, contain lists of the many archives where vital records are kept in Germany. I recommend that you send inquiries to selected addresses, writing down all the dates and facts, and the names of the people you want to know about, and send the information to the addresses that seem most likely to be the place where your ancestral records would be located. This should be done to verify the location before proceeding further with research plans. In many cases it is absolutely necessary to know at least one place where relatives lived, then write to that place (archive or parish). The response will probably be a polite letter telling you to come and have a look yourself.

In former times it was necessary to write in the German language, however, now you may write in English because most Germans who work in archives now know the English language.

Even for people living in Germany trying to trace their ancestry, it can take months of constant working, to find out the name of the homestead where forefathers came from, however, all cases may be different. A search at the Neunkhausen Rathaus turned up the 1843 record of house #30 built by Christian Pfeiffer, giving the precise description and dimensions of the home (See page 126) along with a map of the village showing the location (See page 127).

Neunkhausen Rathaus 1843 Record

[126]

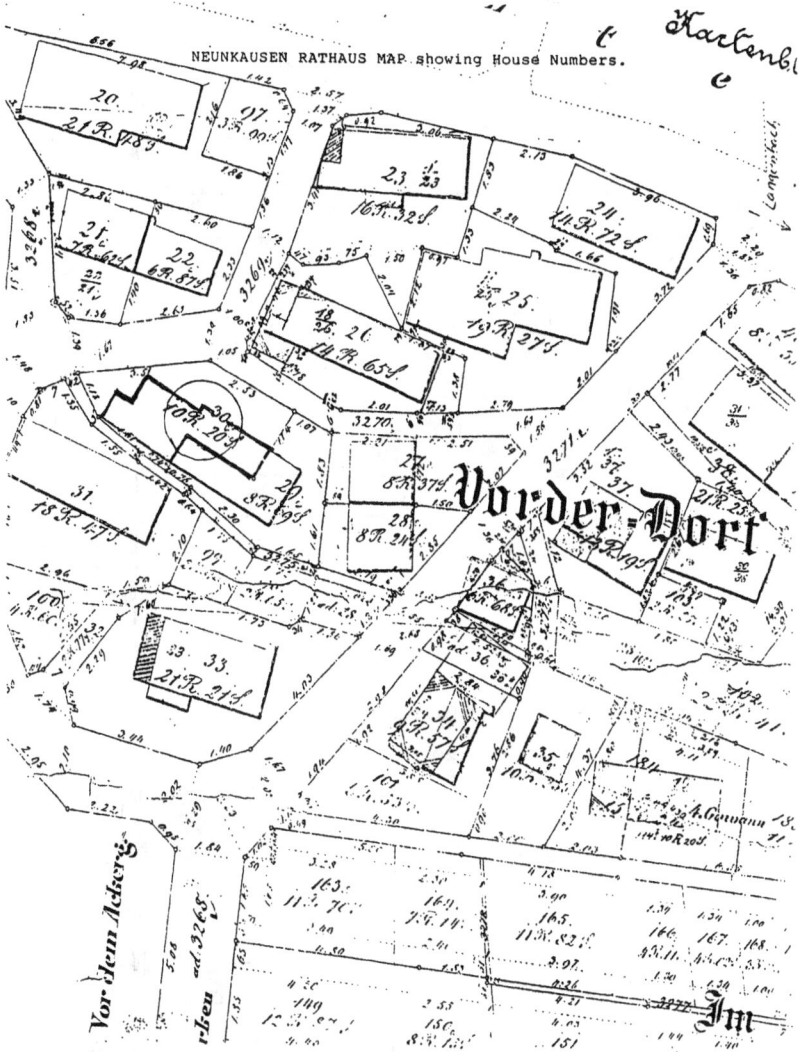

Neunkhausen Rathaus Map

Seite **61**

Nr. *61*

Kirburg am *17 Dezember* 18*82*

Vor dem unterzeichneten Standesbeamten erschien heute, der
Persönlichkeit nach _____
_____ bekannt,

der Landmann Friedrich Wayand

wohnhaft zu *Neunthausen*

evangelischer Religion, und zeigte an, daß von der

Emilie Wayand geborne Pfeiffer

seine Ehefrau

_____ *evangelischer* Religion,

wohnhaft *bei ihm*

zu *Neunthausen in seiner Wohnung*

am _____ *siebenzehnten* Dezember des Jahres

tausend acht hundert *achtzig* zig und *zwei vormittags*

um _____ *drei* Uhr ein Kind *weiblichen*

Geschlechts geboren worden sei, welches _____ *die* _____ Vornamen

Emma

erhalten habe _____

_____

Vorgelesen, genehmigt und *unterschrieben*

Friedrich Wayand

Der Standesbeamte.

H. Maage

Nuenkhausen Civil Birth Register 1882

[128]

Search civil registration, located at the Civil Registry Office, for the following information:

BIRTH REGISTER (*Geburtsregister*; see page 128) - the actual date of birth, since parish records often list only the day of baptism and do not verify birth date. In earlier centuries babies were often baptized on the same day they were born, making it common to assume the baptism date is the actual birth date. Civil vital records searches may be the only means of verifying the name of the parents, as shown in the example on page 120, Kirburg Registry Nr. 61 (Nr. referenced on the Kirburg parish baptism register): Landman Friedrich Weyand of Neunkhausen, Lutheran, notified that Emilie Weyand née Pfeiffer, his wife, Lutheran, living same in his Neunkhausen home, and, Emma, birthdate 16 December 1882 at 3:00 P.M. female child born at Neunkhausen. The name and residence of the person supplying the record may or may not be of interest to the researcher.

MARRIAGE REGISTER (*Eheregister*) - the parish where the wedding took place; names including maiden name of the bride; year and day of birth; residences; occupations of bride and groom; names and occupations of their fathers and mothers; and religion is noted. Civil records of early years are important because they give the name of the father, providing information which can be used to search earlier generations in parish records. See page 118.

Civil marriages must be performed by officials at the *Standesamt* (Office of Vital Records). A second marriage, the church marriage, is permitted afterwards. The civil marriage is the only marriage legally recognized, making it possible for persons of differing confessions to marry.

DEATH REGISTER (*Todesregister/Sterberegister*) - name, place of death, age, occupation of the deceased, cause of death; religion. Sometimes circumstances of death are given; if by violence, there may be court or military records giving further information. Genetic or biological implications of disease are important to the genealogical researcher. Even ancient diagnoses can sometimes be translated into medical terminology by use of medical glossaries so that an educated guess can be made about the cause of death. See page 123.

```
Jahr: 1781  Todestag: 16.2.        Beerd.tag: 18.2.         S./Nr.: 202

Nachh.: Krug                                   geb.:
Vorname: Christian
Geb.Jahr:    0 Geb.tag:                  Alter:   69      Hospitalit: 1
Stand:
Geb.ort: Haina
Wohnung:                                                Hausnr:    0

Vater: Krug
Vorn.Va: Henrich
Va: hiesiger Landsiedler


Mutter:                              gebl:
Vorn.Mu:
Mu:



Ehegatte:                            geb2:
Vorn.Eheg:
Eheg:

Trauungsjahr:    0  Trauungstag:             Konfession:

Todesursache:

Todesort:

Bem: So gegen 40 Jahr in seiner Zelle gelegen.
```

```
                     Day of marriage
Jahr: 1727  Tag d. Trauung: 25.8.          S./Nr.: 273

Nachname: Krug
Vorname: Johannes
Stand Bräutig: Landsiedler  Occ. Settler
Geb.Jahr:    0 Geb.tag: 0   year of birth ; olay
Geb.ort Bräutig: Haina
Wohnung:                                                Hausnr.:   0

Va.Bräutig: bridegroom
Vorn.Va: First name of the father
Vater Brtg.:
Vater Brtg.:

Mu.Bräutig: mother of the bridegroom
Vorn.Mu: First name mother              geb:
Mutter Brtg.:
Mutter Brtg.:

Nachn.Br: Kirchhoff            Second name of bride : Kirchhoff
Vorname Braut: Anna Elisabetha  First name bride: . . . .

Geburtj.Brt:    0 Geb.tag Brt: 0   year, oioy of birth
Geb.ort Br.:
Soz.Stand Brt: Des Aufwärters Johann Kirchhoff Witwe  Occ. Male nurse
Wohng Brt.:            Johann Kirchhoff's Widow    Hausnr.Brt:   0
```

German Genealogy Computer Forms

[130]

Jahr: 1668 S:/Nr.: 7v   Geburtstag: Tauftag: 9.8.

Nachname: Krug
Vorname: Johann Jost
Geburtsort:
Wohnort:
Straße: Hausnr:
Taufstätte:'

Vater: Krug
Vorn.Vater: Jost
Soz.Stand Va:
Herk. Va:

Mutter: geb:
Vorn.Mu:
Soz.Stand Mu:
Herk.Mu:

Pat: Welches Johannes Mebes von Elroda...hoben.

Bem:

Todesjahr: 0   Lebensalter: 0

Jahr: 1657 Tag d.Trauung: 19.11.   S./Nr.: 88r

Nachname: Krug
Vorname: Jost
Stand Bräutig:
Geb.Jahr: 0 Geb.tag: 0
Geb.ort Bräutig: Kirchhaun
Wohnung: Hausnr.:   0

Va.Bräutig:
Vorn.Va:
Vater Brtg.:
Vater Brtg.:

Mu.Bräutig: geb:
Vorn.Mu:
Mutter Brtg.:
Mutter Brtg.:

Nachn.Br: Bornscheuer
Vorname Braut: Anna

Geburtj.Brt: 0 Geb.tag Brt: 0
Geb.ort Br.:
Wohng Brt.:

Va.Brt: Bornscheuer
Vorn.Va Brt: Johannes
Vater Brt.:
Vater Brt.:

Mu.Brt: gebl:
Vorn.Mutter:
Mutter Brt.:
Mutter Brt.:

German Genealogy Computer Forms

[131]

OTHER RECORDS

The computer can be used to find genealogical records in Germany. (See illustrations of genealogical computer printouts, pages 130, 131.) Computer research at Haina Kloster located generations of the Krug family with information dating to 1708.

MUNICIPAL RECORDS

Municipal records hold useful information which can supplement church records. Tax lists, wills from early years (*Testamentes*), records of alms paid to emigrants, and other payments for transportation to America may be researched. Some municipal records begin in the eleventh century, and the information is similar to that which is later found in court records.

COURT RECORDS

The court system in Germany has a trial level and two appellate levels. Court records before 1877 are of many kinds and titles. To obtain a court record it is necessary for the genealogy researcher to determine the jurisidiction to which the person was subject.

POLICE RECORDS

Local police stations have *Melderegisters* (Report Registers) that list all residents and their movements into and out of the area. After World War II it was necessary to obtain a *Zuzuggenehmigung* (permit to move into an area) and *Abmeldeschein* (permit to move away from place of former residence). This makes it possible to trace movements of families after war.

LAND RECORDS

Land Books, called *Grundbucher* in Germany, contain descriptions, ownership, indebtedness, and mortgages of each parcel of land. They are kept in the *Amtsgericht* (Lower Court) of the district in which the parcel of land is located.

OCCUPATIONAL RECORDS

If persons being researched were trained as craftsmen, apprenticed, examined, and certified as a journeyman to travel about the country working for and receiving support of master craftsmen and guilds in other cities, there are extensive guild records that can be searched.

ACADEMIC RECORDS

There are academic records that can be consulted for members of the bourgeoisie, professors, teachers, ministers, lawyers, and physicians.

MILITARY RECORDS

The military records in Germany do not include lists of pensions as can be found for American veterans of war. The military records are not centralized because each principality in Germany recruited its own troops and sold them to any country willing to pay for them, resulting in German military records being found in foreign countries. For example, Hessen military men served in the American Revolution and records of this are in the British Museum as well as in Marburg, Germany. Many military men from Hessen were sold to other countries and the Staatsarchiv in Marburg has gathered records of that area of Germany.

Search for military records:

Staatsarchiv
Friedrichsplatz 15
D-3550 Marburg, Germany

Hauptarchiv
Archivvstrasse 12-14
D-10000 Berlin 33
                Germany

Staatliche Archiv
Kriegsarchiv
Leonrodstrasse 57
D-8000 Munich, Germany

Bundesarchiv
Am Wollerhof 12
D-5400 Koblenz, Germany

In each capital of the states of Germany there is an archive to address inquiries in the English language as follows:

Landesarchiv des Landes
Name of state
Name of capital city, Germany

If writing to a smaller city in the states of Germany, address inquiries in the English language as follows:

Stadtisches Archiv der Stadt
Name of city
Germany

Independent cities in Germany are: Kiel, Hannover, Dusseldorf, Munster, Mainz, Frankfurt, Stuttgart, Munich, Schwerin, Magdeburg, Dresden, Erfurt, Potsdam, Saarbrucken.

Archive locations by states:

BADEN-WURTTEMBERG - Stuttgart, capital city; old university city of Heidelberg; beautiful Lake Constance; famous spa-casino Baden-Baden; and Swabian Forest. Population divided equally between Protestant and Catholic religions. The University of Freiburg Library has a genealogical collection.

Municipal archives in Baden: Stadtsarchiv in Freiburg, Heilbron, Karlsruhe, and Mannheim.

Municipal archives in Württemberg: Stadtarchiv in Goppingen, Ravensberg, Reutkingen, Stuttgart, Tübingen, Ulm.

BAVARIA - Once a kingdom itself; incorporated into the German Empire in 1871. Munich, capital city. Population 3/4 Catholic and 1/4 Protestant. If ancestors were born in what is now Bavaria, they may have been citizens of Austria, France, Prussia or other German states. The Haüpstaatsarchiv (main national archives) is located in Munich at Archivvstrasse 12.

Municipal Archives: Stadtsarchiv in Ansbach, Aschaffenburg, Augsburg, Bamberg, Bayreuth, Donauworth, Erlangen, Fürth, Hof, Inglostadt, Kempton, Kulmbach, Landshut, Munich, Nuremberg, Passau, and Regensberg.

State Archives: Staatsarchiv for Coburg at Schloss Ehrenburg, (Coburg); for Mittelfranken at Nuremburg; for Niederbayern at Landshut; for Oberfranken at Bamberg; for Oberbayern at Munich; for Oberpfalz at Amberg; for Schwaben at Neuberg; for Unterfranken at Würzburg.

BRANDENBURG - Potsdam, capital city. (Berlin is the national capital of Germany.) Area of state formerly known as DDR East Germany. Expansive farmland state known as "breadbasket of Germany." Landesarchiv located in Berlin.
Hauptarchiv
Archivvstrasse 12-14
D-10000 Berlin 33

HESSE - central part of Germany. Wiesbaden, capital city. Name variations throughout history: Hessen-Kassel, Hessen-Darmstadt, Hessen-Marburg, Hessen-Nassau, Kurhessen, Oberhessen, Rhein-Hessen, Fulda, Waldeck. Population 2/3 Protestant, 1/3 Catholic. Cities: Wiesbaden, Frankfurt, Kassel, Fulda. There is not a central archive to search for records.
State Archives: Staatsarchiv at Darmstadt and Marburg
Main State Archive: Haüpstaatsarchiv at Wiesbaden
Municipal Archives: Stadtarchiv in Darmstadt, Frankfurt am Main, Freidburg, Hanau, Kassel, and Wiesbaden.

LOWER SAXONY - northern part of Germany. Bremen, capital city and seaport where many Germans emigrated. Hamburg was port of embarkation for many German immigrants; is largest seaport in the world and has five-hundred foreign consulates. Nine-tenths of population is Protestant, one-tenth Catholic.
State Archives: Staatsarchiv in Bremen, Hamburg, Hannover, Buckeburg, Stade, Oldenburg, Wolfenbuttel, Osnabrück, Aurich, and Göttingen.
Municipal Archives: Stadtarchiv in Buxtehude, Goslar, Helmstedt, Hildesheim, and Hameln.

MECKLENBURG - formerly DDR East Germany. Schwerin, capital city; northern Baltic Sea state bordering Poland.
State Archives: Staatsarchiv in Schwerin, Griefswald.
Municipal Archives: Rostock, Schwerin.

NORTH RHINE-WESTPHALIA - Düsseldorf, capital city. Many emigrants from this state to America in the nineteenth century were listed on passenger lists as Prussians.
State Archives: Staatsarchiv in Münster, Detmold
Main Archives: Haüpstaatsarchiv in Düsseldorf
Passenger List Archives: Personnenstandarchiv in Brühl
Landesamt fur Archiv in Münster
Municipal Archives: Stadtarchiv in Atlens, Bielefeld, Bocholt, Bochum, Bonn, Bottrop, Dortmund, Düsseldorf, Essen, Minden, Münster, Paderborn, Siegen, Soest.

RHINELAND-PALATINATE - borders Belgium, Luxemburg, and France. Mainz, capital city. German emigrants traveled down the Rhine river to Rotterdam to sail for America. Sixty percent of the population is Catholic, forty percent of the population is Protestant. The "Pennsylvania Dutch" Germans emigrated from this state.
Municipal Archives: Stadtarchiv in Mainz

SAAR - region in Saar River basin between France and Germany, once part of Lorraine; became a German state in 1935. Saarbrücken, capital city. State population over one million; 75% Catholic, 25% Protestant.
State Archives: Staatsarchiv in Saarbrücken
Land Archives: Landesarchiv in Saarbrücken
Municipal Archives: Stadtarchiv in Saarbrücken, Volklingen

SAXONY - formerly area of DDR East Germany. Dresden, capital city.
State Archives: Staatsarchiv in Dresden
Municipal Archives: Stadtarchiv in Dresden

SAXONY-ANHALT - formerly area of DDR East Germany. Magdeburg, capital city. Historical city of Leipzig spawned the revolution of 1989 resulting in Berlin Wall coming down and unification of Germany in 1990.
State Archives: Staatsarchiv in Magdeburg, Weimar, Oranienbaum.
Municipal Archives: Stadtarchiv in Magdeburg, Weimar, Halle, Leipzig.
Genealogical institution for research:
Zentralstelle der Genealogie Leipzig
Georgi-Dimitroff-Platz 1
4107 Leipzig, Germany

SCHLESWIG-HOLSTEIN - northernmost part of Germany, former Duchy of Holstein. Kiel, capital city. Population predominantly Saxon Protestants speaking low-German.
Land Archives: Landesarchiv in Schleswig
Municipal Archives: Stadtarchiv in Flensburg, Kiel, Lübeck

THURINGIA - formerly DDR East Germany. Erfurt, capital city. Lutherland historical area; Wartburg Castle and Wittenberg Castle Church famous in Reformation history.
State Archives: Staatsarchiv in Gotha, Meiningen, Rudolstadt.
Municipal Archives: Stadtarchiv in Erfurt, Gotha, Wittenberg.

[7]

Jewish Genealogy Research in Germany

German history refers to Jews having entered Germany with the Romans and two groups of Jews have lived there continuously since that time. Within the Holy Roman Empire German Nation there were various restrictions applied to Jews. Family law determined the number of Jews allowed in a village. Later, in the history of the German Empire, Jews were expelled from the Duchy of Bavaria in 1551 and from the principality of Neuburg in 1671.

Jews in Germany were not members of a community because they were not Christian. They were permitted to live only in designated places and in specified numbers. Jews were subject to their own laws and leaders, and not to the laws of the community in which they lived. The free cities of Germany, after the middle of the fifteenth century, except for a few, prohibited Jewish residents because of competition with gentile businessmen, craftsmen, and the Reformation influence.

The Sephardim (or Maranos) Jews fled Spain and Portugal at the time of the Inquisition in the late fifteenth century. They have Hispanic surnames, a language based on medieval Spanish, and did not intermarry with Ashkenazim Jews in earlier times. The Ashkenazim Jews are descendants of Jews that settled along the Rhine River in Roman times. They speak Yiddish, did not have surnames until the early nineteenth century when the government required them by law, and lived in ghettos because of restrictions. In later centuries they moved to Slavic countries and Poland. The restrictions against Jews were lifted during the first half of the nineteenth century and they became a part of national cultural life in Germany.

Repression of one kind or another shifted the population of Jews in Germany until emigration of Jews to America started in the eighteenth century.

Genealogy has been a Jewish tradition ever since the first chapters of Genesis. Many Jews of German heritage can trace their families back through the generations, possibly into the Middle Ages by probing the memories of living relatives, searching marriage licenses, tombstones dating from A.D. 1077, ships' passenger lists, and birth and death documents in the United States, Germany, and Israel. Family traditions and customs often give clues to a family's ancient origins.

Germany has an organized interest in the past in Jewish genealogy. Jewish-German genealogy has special problems and difficulties that date to the Third Reich and the Holocaust destruction. Searching genealogy today is an attempt to assemble data which has survived the Holocaust. Jewish-German genealogy is well known because of its past use in exterminating Jews and keeping exact records of all Jews who were exterminated. Those records are a valuable German resource today in Jewish genealogy research. The source for locating information about the fate of villages and Holocaust victims kept by the Nazis at concentration camps is called ITS (International Tracing Service), under the auspices of the International Red Cross. There is no charge for research:

International Tracing Service
D-3548 Arolsen
Germany

There are a large number of Jewish birth, death and marriage records existing today in communities of Germany that go back as far as the eighteenth century and earlier.

The Central Archives for the History of the Jewish People in Jerusalem has a large collection of genealogies of German Jews from the twelfth century to the present because the law required German-Jewish communities to keep records. It contains Jewish births, marriages, deaths and tombstone inscriptions in Germany listed by towns between 1800 and 1876. Address:

The Central Archives for the History of the Jewish People
Hebrew University Campus
P. O. Box 1149
Jerusalem, Israel

An English language paper, "Registration of Births, Deaths, and Marriages in European Jewish Communities, in Palestine and in Israel" found in Leslie Pine's *Genealogist's Encyclopedia* contains a survey of the kinds of registration data of Jews in Baden, Bavaria, Braunschweig, Frankfurt, Hamburg, Hannover, Hessen, Hohenzollern-Hechingen, Holstein, Lübeck, Mecklenburg-Schwerin, Oldenburg, Prussia, Saxony, Weimar-Eisenach, Schleswig, Westphalia, and Württemberg. This information dates from 1808 when Napoleon required all Jews of his empire to take family names, and records were kept with a copy turned over to the state. In 1812 the kingdom of Prussia emancipated Jews if they adopted family names.

The Yad Vashem Archives in Jerusalem is visited annually by

many tourists who go to the museum to view the horrors of the Nazi years, 1933-1945, and the collection on Jewish people and communities destroyed during the Nazi Holocaust. Adjoining the museum are buildings containing information for ancestor researchers. The Hall of Names contains information on each of the six million Jewish victims of the Holocaust. If you cannot go in person to Israel, make a written request to the Hall of Names for testimony about a relative who died in the Holocaust that may give further names and clues for family research. The Yad Vashem Archives library reading room has books and archives dealing with the Holocaust period, especially in Eastern Europe where most of the persecution of Jews occurred. If the town from which ancestors came is known, research at the Yad Vashem Archives will be helpful. Memory books (yizkor) from 600 European communities contain lists of Holocaust victims names and dates. Most Jewish libraries in the United States have listings of the documents at Yad Vashem and copies can be ordered by mail by paying all related expenses.

Address: Yad Vashem
P. O. Box 3477
Jerusalem, Israel 91034

In accordance with the Knesset decision of 1985, and the proclamation by the President of Israel, commemorative citizenship was bestowed upon the Jews who perished in the Holocaust, as a symbol of their having been gathered unto their people. Those wishing to receive a certificate of commemorative citizenship in the name of their dear ones who perished should complete a request form (See form, page 141) and write to Yad Vashem Hall of Names at the above address or FAX 433511, 91034 3477

The problems in Jewish genealogy research arise from the fact that it was uncommon for Jews in Germany to have a surname until early in the nineteenth century. After family names became commonly used, persons often changed their names when they moved from one country to another. When names are anglicized in North America it is difficult to trace their origins.

German Jews were among the earliest of Jewish colonists in America. Failure of the 1848 German Revolution in Europe to grant equal rights to Jews caused the migration of many German Jews to the United States. There were large waves of Jewish immigration to North America during the 1840's and 1850's from German states.

A quarterly periodical called "Judische Familienforschung," published 1924-1938 by a society for German-Jewish genealogy, may prove to be a helpful source and is found in most public and state libraries in the United States.

In Germany the state libraries in Berlin, Munich, Hamburg, Frankfurt, and Leipzig have Jewish collections containing many volumes for the genealogy researcher.

Steps in Jewish ancestry research:

1. Talk with a family member who knows the family history.

2. Gather copies: birth, marriage, divorce, and death records.

3. Search synagogue and cemetery records.

4. Scan immigration and naturalization records and ships' passenger lists.

5. Search federal census and military records.

6. Look up city directories that may list family members.

7. Hunt for newspaper obituaries that give clues to family.

8. Check Israeli sources for names and clues in Germany.

9. Contact German civil registry offices in cities near family origin.

10. Contact German parish registers in village of family origin.

YAD VASHEM

Martyrs' and Heroes'
Remembrance Authority
P.O.B. 3477 Jerusalem, Israel

דף-עד
עדות-בלאט
A Page of Testimony

יד ושם

אינסטיטוט צום אנדענק
פון אומקום און גבורה

THE MARTYRS' AND HEROES'
REMEMBRANCE LAW, 5713–1953
determines in article No. 2 that –

The task of YAD VASHEM is to gather into the homeland material regarding all those members of the Jewish people who laid down their lives, who fought and rebelled against the Nazi enemy and his collaborators, and to perpetuate their NAMES and those of the communities, organisations, and institutions which were destroyed because they were Jewish.

דאס געזעץ אנדענק פון אומקום און גבורה - יד-ושם, תשי"ג 1953
שטעלט פעסט אין פאראגראף נומי 2 :

די אויפגאבע פון יד-ושם איז איינצואמלען אין היימלאנד דעם אנדענק פון אלע יידן, וואס זענען געפאלן, האבן זיך מוסר נפש געווען, געקעמפט און זיך אנטקעגנגעשטעלט דעם נאצישן שונא און זיינע אויסהעלפער, און זיי אלעמען, די קהילות, די ארגאניזאציעס און אינסטיטוטוציעס, וועלכע זענען חרוב געווארן צוליב זייער אנגעהעריקייט צום יידישן פאלק — שטעלן א דענקמאל.
(געזעץ-בוך נומי 231, י"ד אלול תשי"ג, 3.8.82.)

DETAILS OF VICTIM: INSCRIBE EACH VICTIM ON A SEPARATE PAGE, IN BLOCK LETTERS
דאטען וועגן אומגעקומענעם: יעדן נאמען אויף א באזונדער בלאט, מיט קלארער שריפט

Family name:	1. פאמיליע-נאמען:
First name:	2. פארנאמען:
Previous name: (nee for woman)	3. פאמיליע-נאמען פאר דער חתונה (פאר א פרוי):

Victim's photo write victim's name on back side please

בילד פון דעם אומגעקומענעם שרייבט או דעם נאמען אויף דער ריקזייט פון דעם בילד

6. פארהיירַאט! Fam. status	5. מין Sex	4. געבורטס-דאטע (ווי אלט) Birth date or appr. age

Birth place and country:	7. ארט פון געבורט (שטאט, לאנד):

| Victim's mother | - First name: | 8. מוטער פון דעם |
| | - Maiden name/nee: | - פארנאמען: אומגעקומענעם - מיידלשע-פאמיליע: |

| Victim's father | - First name: | 9. פאטער פון דעם |
| | | - פארנאמען: אומגעקומענעם |

| Victim's spouse | - First name: | 10. מאן/פרוי פון |
| | - Maiden name/nee: | - פארנאמען: דעם אומגעקומענעם - מיידלשע-פאמיליע: |

Permanent residence place and country:	11. סטאביליער וואוינארט (שטאט, לאנד):

Wartime residence place and country:	12. וואוינערטער בעת דער מלחמה (שטאט, לאנד):

Date/year of death:	14. צייט פון טויט:	Victim's profession:	13. ברוף אדער פאך:

Death place: Circumstances of death:	15. ארט און אומשטענדן פון טויט:

Reported by: געשריבן פון:

I, the undersigned _____ איך, דער אונטערגעשריבענער

Residing at (address) _____ וואס וואוינט (אדרעס)

Relationship to victim (family/other) _____ קרובישאפט

HEREBY DECLARE THAT THIS TESTIMONY IS CORRECT TO THE BEST OF MY KNOWLEDGE
דערקלער דערמיט, אז די עדות מיט אלע פרטים איז א ריכטיקע לויט מיין בעסטען וויסן

Place and date _____ ארט און דאטע Signature _____ אונטערשריפט

"...ונתתי להם בביתי ובחומתי יד ושם..אשר לא יכרת". ישעיהו נו ה

"...even unto them will I give in mine house and within my walls a place and a name...that shall not be cut off." isaiah, lvi,5

Yad Vashem form

[141]

YAD VASHEM
Instituto de Conmemoración
de los Mártires y de los Héroes
P.O.B. 3477 Jerusalén, Israel

Hoja de Testimonio

דף–עד
עדות–בלאט

יד ושם
אינסטיטוט צום אנדענק
פון אומקום און גבורה

LA LEY PARA CONMEMORAR A LOS
MARTIRES Y LOS HEROES, 5713-1953
manifiesta en el artículo 2 :
La función de Yad Vashem es registrar y
reunir en Israel el recuerdo de todos los
judíos que perecieron o que cayeron
luchando contra el enemigo nazi y sus
cómplices, para perpetuar sus
NOMBRES y los de las comunidades,
instituciones y organizaciones que fueron
destruídas por haber pertenecido al
pueblo judío.

דאס געזעץ אנדענק פון אומקום און גבורה - יד-ושם, תשי"ג 1953
שטעלט פעסט אין פאראגראף נומ' 2 :
די אויפגאבע פון יד-ושם איז איינצאמלען אין היימלאנד דעם
אנדענק פון אלע יידן, וואס זענען געפאלן, האבן זיך מוסר נפש
געווען, געקעמפט און זיך אנטקעגנגעשטעלט דעם נאצישן שונא און
זיינע ארויסהעלפער, און זיי אלעמען, די קהילות, די ארגאניזאציעס
און אינסטיטוציעס, וועלכע זענען חרוב געווארן צוליב זייער
אנגעהעריקייט צום יידישן פאלק — שטעלן א דענקמאל.
(געזעץ-בוך נומ' 231, י"ז אלול תשי"ג, 82.8.3591)

דאטען וועגן אומגעקומענעם: יעדן נאמען אויף א באזונדער בלאט, מיט קלארער שריפט
DATOS DE LA VICTIMA: INSCRIBIR CADA VICTIMA EN UN FORMULARIO SEPARADO, CON MAYUSCULAS

בילד פון דעם אומגעקומענעם שרייבט אז דעם נאמען אויף דער ריקזייט פון דעם בילד Foto de la víctima escriba el nombre de la víctima en el revés de la foto	Apellido:	1. פאמיליע-נאמען:
	Nombre:	2. פארנאמען:
	Apellido previo (de soltera):	3. פאמיליע-נאמען פאר דער חתונה (פאר א פרוי):
	5. מין 6. פארהייראט! Sexo Estado fam.	4. געבורטס-דאטע (ווי אלט) Fecha nacimiento/edad
	Lugar y país de nacimiento:	7. ארט פון געבורט (שטאאט, לאנד):
Madre de la - Nombre: víctima - Apellido de soltera:	- פארנאמען: - מיידלשע-פאמיליע:	8. מוטער פון דעם אומגעקומענעם
Padre de - Nombre: la víctima	- פארנאמען:	9. פאטער פון דעם אומגעקומענעם
Esposo/a de - Nombre: la víctima - Apellido de soltera:	- פארנאמען: - מיידלשע-פאמיליע:	10. מאן/פרוי פון דעם אומגעקומענעם
Domicilio permanente lugar y país:		11. שטאביליער וואוינארט (שטאאט, לאנד):
Domicilio durante la guerra lugar y país:		12. וואוינערטער בעת דער מלחמה (שטאאט, לאנד):
Fecha/año del fallecimiento:	14. צייט פון טויט:	Profesión de la víctima:	13. בערוף אדער פאך:
Lugar del fallecimiento: Circunstancias del fallecimiento:		15. ארט און אומשטעטנדן פון טויט:

Registrado por: _____ גערשריבן פון:

Yo, el/la firmante _____ איך, דער אונטערגעשריבענער

Dirección completa _____ וואס וואוינט (אדרעס)

Parentesco/relación con el difunto _____ קרובישאפט

דערקלער דערמיט, אז די עדות מיט אלע פרטים איז א ריכטיקע לויט מיין בעסטען וויסן
DECLARO QUE ESTE TESTIMONIO ES FIEL Y DE ACUERDO A MI MEJOR CONOCIMIENTO

Fecha y lugar _____ ארט און דאטע   Firma _____ אונטערשריפט

"...ונתתי להם בביתי ובחומותי יד ושם..אשר לא יכרת". ישעיהו נו ה
"...les daré en mi casa y mis muros trofeo y
renombre... que no desaparecerá." Isaías, LVI, 5

Yad Vashem form, Spanish language

[142]

[8]

Making A Family History Workbook

If you have taken on the challenge of genealogy research to trace your ancestors in Germany, you may one day be the ancestor that made it possible for future generations of your family to construct a complete family tree. If any of your ancestors had taken the time and energy to record information about your family, you would now have a more complete family tree than you are able to reconstruct by starting out without any information.

You can be the one who links the current generation of your family with history by sharing names, dates, stories, and photographs. You have the opportunity to discover the ancestral family homes, the cemeteries, and stories about emigration and immigration to America.

Preserve your genealogical experiences by forming them into a workbook that can be expanded with new information as time goes by. Once you have searched in Germany, you will continue to find new clues and gather additional new insights that will be of interest to members of your family in future generations. The collection of material in your workbook will continue to expand as years go by. New discoveries require an organized way of looking back at collected family history. The author's recent research of a German history book revealed the Krug surname dated in the year 1301 when they were a family of knights residing in the village of Moischeid, Germany. This new discovery of a fourteenth-century family history requires an in-depth understanding of German history at that time and continued family research.

There are as many ways of organizing family history and mementos of research as there are genealogy searchers. The amount of information you have gathered will make a difference in deciding the best way to preserve your family's history. If you decide to continue searching sibling branches of the family line, your workbook should be set up right from the beginning as a framework for a more extensive family history.

Use of a computer genealogy program makes it possible to store large amounts of genealogical information, however, there is no substitute for being able to look at that information in printed form to examine and compare data such as names, dates, etc. A plan that coordinates computer and notebook storage, if it is possible to have access to a computer program, is probably the best method and the most practical way to keep family history over a period of years.

The reward for organizing your research and writing your family history is that it points the way for future research plans. Missing information is easily spotted. Ideas begin to formulate for adding methods to obtain complete information.

Here is a suggested outline for organizing a family history workbook that is flexible, and may be expanded to meet individual needs:

I. Begin with your immigrant ancestor(s). Gather together all the information collected about the immigrant ancestor -- photographs, marriage certificate, death certificate, obituary, photocopies of birth registration in Germany, and any other registrations in Germany such as confirmation. This preserves the primary sources you have researched. Include a map of the location of the residence in Germany and any other descriptive information collected when researching genealogy in Germany. If your German family history branches out to more families from Germany, this section may need to become a separate and complete workbook on just the subject of German immigrants in your family.

II. The settling of your German family in America. A collection of historical facts and documents about the occupation and residence of your immigrant family in America. If the family moved from one state to another, write a narrative telling what you know about their life. Add the oral tradition you have collected from other family members and that of their descendants tracing family history to you, the author of the family history. Photographs and maps, clippings from newspapers, and family memorabilia make this an interesting part of your family history workbook. If this historical collection is voluminous, this section may also become a separate and complete workbook in itself, organized so additions may be made from time to time.

III. The family tree. Your completed pedigree chart and generation lineage charts belong in this section. Include the table of consanguinity worked out with your family names. This part of the workbook is bound to change over the years as new information develops about your family history. It is a good idea to make this information into a separate workbook that can easily be picked up and taken anywhere, and anytime the opportunity arises to do genealogy research.

IV. A research log listing all the sources you have searched. Itemize specific dates of mailings and dates of responses received. Without this information over the years it is very easy to forget what has been done on a particular item of genealogy research, or when the information was received that you have forgotten about. Additionally, some researchers prefer to keep a separate research journal detailing progress on each person searched. Record all the names, dates, and places you discover. List approximate dates until exact dates are found through further research.

V. Collect all the miscellaneous information and material gathered which may or may not be important in other sections of your workbook. Include conflicting information, and questions raised by relatives. Keep notations about helpful references that may be sought out in future research. The is the place to note research goals about information you would like to find or verify.

SUMMARY: A family history workbook can be a permanent record or it can be a place to record information that will be used in other ways. Researching genealogy in Germany requires organization, to identify the name and residence of the immigrant ancestor(s) and to continue searching. Since German history originates in antiquity, a family history workbook makes it possible to continue genealogical searching indefinitely. Accurate recording of all information, both before and during research in Germany, can lead to a rewarding encounter with Germanic heritage and European roots that unites past ancestors with the present generation.

Bibliography

Eichholy, Alice, Ed., *Ancestry's Redbook.* Salt Lake City: 1992.

Baxter, Angus, *In Search Of Your German Roots. A Complete Guide To Tracing Your Ancestors In The Germanic Areas Of Europe.* Baltimore: Genealogical Publishing Co., Inc. 1991.

Bentz, Edna M., *If I Can You Can Decipher Germanic Records.* San Diego: 1991.

Byler, John M. *Amish Immigrants of Waldeck and Hesse.* Bellville Ohio: (Elverson, Pennsylvania, Olde Springfield Shop) 1993.

Fulbrook, Mary, *A Concise History of Germany.* New York: Cambridge University Press, 1991.

Glazier, Ira A. and P. William Filby, *Germans to America: Lists of Passengers Arriving at U.S. Ports 1850-1895,* Wilmington: Scholarly Resources, 1988-1994.

Greenwood, Val D., *The Researcher's Guide To American Genealogy.* Baltimore: Genealogical Publishing Co., Inc. 1990.

Jacob, Otto, *Löhlbach ein Bergdorf im Kellerwald 1200 Year History.* Kassel, Germany: 1988.

Jones, George F., *German-American Names.* Baltimore: Genealogical Publishing Co., Inc., 1990.

Kemp, Thomas Jay, *International Vital Records Handbook.* Baltimore: Genealogical Publishing Co., Inc. 1990.

Kretschmer, Albert, *Das grosse Buch der Volkstrachten.* Eltville am Rhein, Germany: Rheingauer Verlagsgesellschaft, 1982.

Palen, Margaret Krug, *Genealogical Research Guide to Germany.* Bowie, Maryland: Heritage Books, Inc., 1988.

Palen, Margaret Krug. *German Settlers of Iowa, Their Descendants, and European Ancestors.* Bowie, Maryland: Heritage Books, Inc., 1994.

Pine, L. G. *The Genealogist's Encyclopedia.* New York: Collier Books, 1970.

Thode, Ernest. *The Address Book for Germanic Genealogy.* Baltimore: Genealogical Publishing Co., Inc., 1991.

Tolzmann, Don Heinrich. *Upper Midwest German Biographical Index.* Bowie, Maryland: Heritage Books, Inc., 1993.

Zug, John D. Zug and Karin Gottier, Editors, *German-American Life.* Monticello, Iowa: Julin Printing Company, 1991.

Glossary

Alamanni: Germanic tribe in territory now called Baden-Wurttemberg.

Anglo-American: a resident of the United States whose language, ancestry, and culture are English.

Anglo-Saxon: a descendant of Germanic tribes (Angles, Saxons, and Jutes) that settled in Britain in the fifth and sixth centuries and were dominant until the Norman Conquest of 1066; any person of English ancestry.

Augsburg Confession: The 1530 diet of the rulers of the Holy Roman Empire convoked by Emperor Charles V required Protestants to state differences with the Roman Church. Religious reformer Melanchthon composed articles of faith and doctrine or justification recounting abuses in religious practices corrected by Protestants.

Baroque: any work, building or sculpture in the architectural style that was developed in Europe about 1550 to 1750, composed of elaborate and ornate scrolls, curves, and powerful interlocking forms.

Burgundians: Germanic tribe of duchy region of southwestern France.

Celts: ancient people of western and central Europe including Gaul.

Cenotaph: tomb or monument to honor dead person/groups buried elsewhere.

Ciborium: canopy over high altar; often in form of a dome supported by columns.

Consanguinity: blood relationship; descended from the same ancestor.

Count: in Germany a nobleman whose rank corresponds to that of an earl in England.

Crypt: burial place; churches often were built above an old crypt.

Duchy: the territory ruled by a duke or duchess; a dukedom.

Duke: in Germany a prince, ruler of an independent duchy.

Eheregister: wedding register.

Fachverk: German half-timbered architecture; heavy beam construction with infill of loam or brick.

First Reich: the government of the German empire during the Holy Roman Empire period from the ninth century to 1806.

Flying Buttress: half-arches and arches strengthening outer walls of cathedrals with very large Gothic windows.

Franks: Germanic tribe of Rhine region in early Christian era that conquered Gaul about 500 A.D. and established an extensive empire that reached its greatest power in the ninth century; divided into subgroups of which many were Palatines who emigrated to America in the eighteenth century.

Frauenkirche: Church of Our Lady.

Fresco: the art of painting pigments without bonding agents applied to moist lime plaster.

Frieze: decorative borders of a wall, two- or three-dimensional, consisting of figures or ornaments.

Frisii: Germanic North Sea tribe.

Gable: triangular upper section of a wall; usually found at end of pitched roof; may be purely decorative.

Gaul: ancient name of region in Europe south and west of the Rhine, west of the Alps, and north of the Pyrenees; the territory of modern France and Belgium.

Geburtsregister: birth register.

Generation: a group of individuals constituting a single step in the line of descent from an ancestor.

Goths: Germanic tribe originally settled between the Elbe and Vistula Rivers, who invaded the Roman Empire in the early centuries of the Christian era.

Gothic: Middle Ages period of European art and architecture from mid-twelfth century to the sixteenth century characterized by the medieval lancet arch.

Hanseatic League: From the thirteenth to the seventeenth centuries, German merchants in two-hundred towns including Bergen, Norway, and Novgorod, Russia, formed a confederation bound by a common language, legal system, currency and traditions of civic and individual rights.

Huguenots: French Reformed Protestants of the sixteenth and seventeenth centuries; adherents of a Swiss political movement opposing annexation by the Duke of Savoy.

Kloster: cloister; monastery.

Kreis: county; district.

Landgrave: in medieval Germany, the title of certain princes; a count who had jurisdiction over a particular territory.

Landgravine: the wife of a landgrave; female ruler.

Lend-Lease: the aid program during World War II through which the United States provided food, munitions, and goods to countries whose defense against Germany and Italy was considered necessary to the United States according to the Lend-Lease Act passed March 11, 1941.

Lineage: descent in a line from a common ancestor.
Lombards: Elbe Germanic tribe of origin in northern Italy.
Luftmaleri: paintings on walls, particularly in south Germany.
Mansard: angled roof which has lower slope steeper than the upper.
Margrave: hereditary title of certain princes in the Holy Roman Empire; the lord of a medieval German border province.
Margravine: the wife or widow of a margrave.
Monstrance: ornamented container in which the consecrated Host is placed; often carried in religious festivals and parades.
Necronyms: reuse of deceased sibling's names.
Obelisk: pillar with square ground and pyramidal peak.
Onion dome: bulbous dome with a point in Germany, Russia and Eastern Europe.
Orangery: part of Baroque castles and parks originally intended to shelter orange trees and other plants in winter.
Palatinate: the region west of the Rhine River, now the state of Rheinland-Palatinate which began to figure in German history in the eleventh century.
Principality: a territory ruled by a prince, from which a prince derives his title or jurisdiction.
Progenitor: direct ancestor; originator of a line of descent.
Rathaus: city hall.
Renaissance: Italian art and architecture from the early fifteenth century to the mid-sixteenth century; it came at the end of the medieval time and was the beginning of a new view based on classical antiquity.
Rococo: design style at the end of the Baroque period (1720-70) characterized by extravagant and elaborate, elegant oval forms.
Romanesque: architectural style from 1000-1300 distinguished by round arches and heavy general appearance.
Sarcophagus: stone coffin, often richly decorated.
Saxons: Germanic tribal group inhabiting northern Germany who invaded and conquered England with the Angles and Jutes in the fifth century A.D.
Second Reich: the German Empire, 1871-1919; the Weimar Republic, 1919-1933.
Sibling: one or more individuals having common parent(s).
Sterberegister: death register.
Stufengiebel: step-gable architecture of northern Germany, Holland, and Belgium.
Taufregister: baptism or christening register.
Third Reich: the government of the German Empire, 1933-1945.
Todesregister: death register.
Transept: part of church at right angles to central aisle (nave).
Trauregister: marriage register.

Triptych: pictures or carvings in three panels side by side and hinged together; a religious story used as an altarpiece with a central panel and two flanking panels half its size that fold over it.

Ubii: ancient Germanic tribe of what is now the city of Cologne.

Vandals: Germanic tribe that overran Gaul, Spain, and northern Africa in the fourth and fifth centuries A.D., and sacked Rome in 455 A.D.; Germanic "vandal" means "wanderer."

Westphalia: formerly a Prussian province north of the State of Hesse, lying between the Weser and the Rhine Rivers.

Zwinger: in the Baroque period, the area between the inner and outer walls of medieval town fortifications used for recreation.

Index